Assessing the Impact of Input Enhancement in Second Language Education

Evolution in Theory, Research and Practice

Edited by Carolyn Gascoigne

Stillwater, Oklahoma
U.S.A.

NEW FORUMS PRESS INC.

Published in the United States of America
by New Forums Press, Inc.1018 S. Lewis St.
Stillwater, OK 74074
www.newforums.com

Copyright © 2007 by New Forums Press, Inc.

All rights reserved. No part of this publication may be reproduced or transmitted in any form or by any means, electronic or mechanical, including photocopy, or any information storage or retrieval system, without permission in writing from the publisher.

Library of Congress Cataloging-in-Publication Data Pending

This book may be ordered in bulk quantities at discount from New Forums Press, Inc., P.O. Box 876, Stillwater, OK 74076 [Federal I.D. No. 73 1123239]. Printed in the United States of America.

ISBN-13: 978-1-581071-23-8
ISBN-10: 1-58107-123-X

Printed in the United States of America.

Table of Contents

Introduction v
    Carolyn Gascoigne, *University of Nebraska at Omaha*

Chapter 1. A History of Input Enhancement: Defining
an Evolving Concept.. 1
    Charlene Polio, *Michigan State University*

Chapter 2. Salience as a Concept in Cognitive Psychology ... 19
    Roger J. Kreuz, *University of Memphis*
    Gina M. Caucci, *University of Memphis*

Chapter 3. Input Enhancement in Classroom-Based SLA
Research: An Attentional Perspective............................... 37
    Ronald P. Leow, *Georgetown University*

Chapter 4. Focus on Form Through Recasts in Dyadic
Student-Teacher Interaction: A Case
for Recast Enhancement 53
    Hossein Nassaji, *University of Victoria*

Chapter 5. Saliency in Second Language Listening
and Reading 71
    Mark H. Overstreet, *Dickinson College*

Chapter 6. Processing Instruction and Structured Input
as Input Enhancement... 89
    Wynne Wong, *Ohio State University*

Chapter 7. The Role of Interaction in Input Enhancement ... 107
    Jessica Williams, *University of Illinois at Chicago*
    Claudia Fernández, *DePaul University*

Chapter 8. Complementary Roles for Input and Output Enhancement in Form-Focused Instruction 129
    Roy Lyster, McGill University

Chapter 9. Input Enhancement by Natural Language Processing 153
    Noriko Nagata, University of San Francisco

Chapter 10. Some Thoughts on The Future of Research on Input Enhancement 169
    Bill VanPatten, University of Illinois at Chicago

Introduction
Carolyn Gascoigne, University of Nebraska at Omaha

Initially, proponents of consciousness raising/input enhancement (CR/IE) dared to promote the notion of selectively focusing on form during the height of the communicative competence revolution by suggesting that an increase in the salience of target grammatical features can facilitate language acquisition. Currently, the influence of CR/IE can be felt in the study of contemporary notions such as salience, noticing, attention, detection, orientation, vividness, awareness, and metalanguage, as well as in the development of principle methods and techniques such as processing instruction, focus on form, and whole language. As the debate over how to treat second language (L2) grammar rages on—often swinging between extreme implicit and explicit positions—it is important to consider and acknowledge the contributions of input enhancement theory on the promotion of intermediate positions that seek to create a meaningful fusion of communication and form.

Because they are extensive and varied, aspects of input enhancement in research and in the classroom often go undetected. Pausing to assess the implications of input enhancement and assemble a body of theory and research will provide a valuable resource to researchers and practitioners who are now considering the role of salience, attention, and awareness in the study of L2 grammar and general second language acquisition (SLA). To this end, this volume assembles a timely, representative selection of opinions and research on input enhancement written by the most prominent scholars in the field of second language research and teaching that examines the influence of input enhancement theory and its permutations on current SLA theory and practice. It is also intended to serve as an ancillary textbook for L2 methods courses, as it contains *Questions and Topics for Discussion* related to each chapter.

In Chapter 1 Charlene Polio provides a contextual backdrop for considering the development and evolution of input enhancement, as well as a clarification of terms. Roger Kreuz and Gina Caucci expand the historical context in Chapter 2 to include discussions of salience and attention as concepts in cognitive psychology, and the relationships between SLA and cognitive theory and research. In Chapter 3 Ronald Leow discusses the role of attention and awareness in classroom-based SLA research, and in Chapter 4 Hossein Nassaji provides an example of classroom-based research using the recast as a form of input enhancement. In Chapter 5 Mark Overstreet looks at input enhancement in listening and reading environments. In Chapter 6 Wynne Wong reviews input enhancement as accomplished through structured input and processing instruction, while Jessica Williams and Claudia Fernández assess its impact on and in classroom interaction in Chapter 7. In Chapter 8 Roy Lyster reviews the role of input (and output) enhancement in form-focused instruction. In Chapter 9 Noriko Nagata looks at technology as a means of input enhancement. Finally, in Chapter 10, Bill VanPatten takes a look back before contemplating the future of research on input enhancement and the implications thereof.

About the Editor

Carolyn Gascoigne holds a PhD in French and Second Language Acquisition from Florida State University and is an associate professor and chair of the Department of Foreign Languages at the University of Nebraska at Omaha.

She has published over 40 refereed articles on various facets of the language teaching and learning process, edited a volume on foreign language program articulation, and authored a book on the changing role grammar in the second language classroom.

Chapter 1
A History of Input Enhancement: Defining an Evolving Concept

Charlene Polio, Michigan State University

If an adult listens to radio broadcasts in a never-before-heard language, it is uncontroversial that even after many hours, the adult will not have learned any of the new language. Larsen-Freeman and Long (1991), citing relevant empirical studies, claimed this to be the case for children as well. Indeed, no method in the history of language teaching has advocated mere exposure to the target language, which indicates agreement that ambient input is not sufficient for adult language learning to occur.

Krashen (1981, 1982; Krashen & Terrell, 1983) proposed that learners needed only input at the initial stages of language learning. Even Krashen, however, eventually argued that input alone was not enough: something had to be done to the input to make it comprehensible. A language teacher, through pictures, gestures, and language modifications could, Krashen argued, help the learner understand and acquire the language implicitly. One interpretation of Krashen's view is that the teacher's job is to enhance input to make it comprehensible. Pointing to a picture while uttering a word, gesturing an action while using a new verb, or simply repeating a word in isolation are all activities that will help a language learner process difficult language, and are examples of input enhancement. In fact, the primary role of the teacher in most language teaching methods is to do something to the input. If it were not, teachers would not be necessary. The language teacher is an input enhancer. Most teachers and researchers today reject Krashen's views of second language acquisition, not because of what he said needed to be done to the input, but because of his dismissal of other techniques that could help learners, such as explicit rules and the facilitative effect of various types of negative feedback. Indeed, many researchers have argued and demonstrated empirically that comprehensible input alone is not enough—most noteably Long (e.g., 1981, 1983, 1996, 2000), who said that interaction and an implicit focus on language form was needed for second language acquisition, and Swain (e.g., 1985, 1995, 2005), who said that modified input alone was not sufficient for achieving grammatical accuracy and that learners had to produce language as well. More recently, others (Ellis, 2001; Norris & Ortega, 2000) have concluded that an *explicit* focus on language is facilitative of second language acquisition. Hence, the nature of what needs to be done to the input has changed, but everyone agrees that something has to be done to it. In discussing what needs to be done, many authors and researchers have used the term input enhancement.

Defining Input Enhancement

In the field of second language acquisition and second language teaching, many specialized terms are widely used but not uniformly defined. Sometimes this phenomenon happens because a term is not well defined in its initial usage. The terms *communicative language teaching* and a *process approach to writing* may be representative examples. More often, a term is explicitly and clearly defined, but then changes as new researchers and authors begin to use it and adopt a less restricted definition. **Task-based language teaching** is one such example. Long's (Long, 2000; Long & Crookes, 1992) original use of the term was restricted to a particular kind of task, one associated with the real world, but now many authors use it to refer to a wide variety of pedagogical tasks. Although these shifting definitions are perhaps inevitable in any field, researchers and teachers need to have a common vocabulary if they are to communicate effectively with one another. All authors need to be explicit about their definitions of any second language acquisition jargon.

The term **input enhancement** (IE) is no exception to this array of confusing constructs. To complicate matters, the term **focus on**

form (FonF) has come into fashion causing people to wonder about the overlap of the two terms. What makes these two terms difficult to disentangle is that the term *IE* has become more narrow, whereas the term *FonF* has broadened in the past ten years. The purpose of this chapter is to present an historical sketch of IE in the endeavor of language teaching. Inherent in such a presentation is a detailed discussion of what exactly IE is. We need to understand what the term first meant and what it now means if we, as language teachers and researchers, are to have fruitful dialogues about the role of IE in language teaching and learning. Furthermore, with other concepts such as FonF, not to mention focus on forms (FonFS) and form-focused instruction (FFI), being used, we need to deconstruct these labels as well and determine how they both resemble and differ from IE.

From Consciousness-Raising to Input Enhancement

Early methods of language teaching such as the grammar translation and the audiolingual method advocated providing learners with explicit grammar rules. The direct approach, encouraging all instruction in the target language, and Krashen and Terrell's (1983) Natural Approach were the first to place emphasis on large amounts of input. As discussed above, although Krashen did argue that something had to be done to the input, it was ironically Michael Sharwood Smith, who argued against Krashen's views, and who was the first to use the term *input enhancement* and promote its importance in language learning. Sharwood Smith (1991) coined the term in an attempt to refine an earlier term, **consciousness-raising** (CR), from Sharwood Smith (1981).

Consciousness-raising, when first mentioned, was not explicitly defined in Sharwood Smith (1981). Instead, he said that CR was not the type of rule memorization associated with the grammar translation method. Rather, CR was broader and could vary with regard to the degree of explicitness and the degree of elaboration involved. (These terms are discussed below.) Based on arguments by Bialystok (1981) and McLaughlin (1978), Sharwood Smith concluded that there was "no reason to assume that consciousness-raising by the teacher and conscious learning by the learner cannot be investigated in a systematic way using some less simplistic model as a guide" (p. 167), the less simplistic model being the one proposed by Krashen.

Later, Sharwood Smith (1991) summarized his discussion of CR stating that he had characterized it as "a deliberate focus on the formal properties of language with a view to facilitating the development of L2 knowledge" (p. 119). At this time, he also decided to abandon the term CR because, he claimed, it was misleading. It did not address the issue of what consciousness was, a term that many cognitive psychologists preferred not to use or define. Sharwood Smith then proposed the term **input enhancement** because it focused on what was being done to the input, not on what was happening in the mind of the learner. He defined it as, "the process by which language input becomes salient to the learner" (p. 119).

Meanwhile, although Sharwood Smith suggested, in a well-justified move, eliminating the term *consciousness-raising*, it remained and was used by Fotos (1993) to refer to a communicative activity that had grammar as the focus of its content. Such tasks are described in detail in Fotos and Ellis (1991). In one example, ESL students got into groups and each received different information about dative alternation with various English verbs. Together, they had to complete a worksheet on rules for dative alternation. The rationale for such a task was that it was both communicative, in that the students had to exchange information to complete the task, and grammar focused in that a specific rule was to be learned and had to be articulated by the learners. Both Fotos (1993) and Fotos and Ellis (1991) concluded that such tasks were useful and promoted learners' noticing of targeted structures. Results of any studies of the effectiveness of such techniques need to be interpreted cautiously. For example, the measures used to assess learning may not ensure that learners can use the structures in spontaneous speech. Nevertheless, some optimism for the benefits of such tasks is reasonable.

In Doughty and Williams' (1998) seminal volume on focus on form, they included consciousness-raising as one type of FonF distinctly different from IE and they defined CR tasks as those used by Fotos (1993). They defined IE as a type of typographical change, such as boldfacing, or phonological change, such as stress or volume, which is now often what many people assume IE to be. But if we return to Sharwood Smith (1991), we will see that he did not define the term so narrowly.

Sharwood Smith's Definition of Input Enhancement

Sharwood Smith (1991) suggested that CR was a misleading term because it focused on the internal state of learner, that is, it implied that the learner was becoming conscious (ignoring exactly what that meant) of structure. Input enhancement, rather, highlighted "the operation that is carried out on the linguistic material" (p. 120). He went on to say that "what we are talking about when dealing with the phenomenon of consciousness-raising is induced input salience and not salience that is naturally occurring" (p. 121). These comments indicated that input enhancement was an external process, an intervention so to speak. Indeed, Sharwood Smith, repeating ideas from his 1981 CR article, classified these interventions along two dimensions, elaboration and explicitness.

Elaboration refers to the length of the operation, that is, what is being done to the input. For example, if an instructor gives one short explanation when a learner error occurs, that is considered less elaborate than if the instructor gives a long explanation every time the error occurs. The variable of elaboration is mentioned by Williams (2005) in her discussion of form-focused instruction, classifying different types of FonF as to whether or not they are *brief*. In her terminology, +brief would be the same as -elaborate.

Another example that illustrates this variable is a recast (-elaborate or +brief) as opposed to a correction with an explanation of the error (+elaborate or -brief). A recast is not elaborate because the interlocutor simply rephrases the learner's utterance with the correct structure and continues on with the interaction. An explanation of the error would last longer and thus be considered elaborate. But these two techniques also vary according to explicitness. According to Sharwood Smith (1991), **explicitness** has to do with the "sophistication and detail" (p. 119) of the process. He gave the example of a signal when an error occurs (-explicit) as opposed to a short explanation (+explicit). The concept of *sophistication* seems difficult to operationalize, and *detail* certainly overlaps with the concept of *elaboration*; the more detailed something is the more elaborate it will be as well.

Although the degree of explicitness is undoubtedly an important concept and one mentioned by Williams (2005) in her taxonomy, it is important to understand that there is little agreement on the term *explicit* either. One widely used definition of explicit is from DeKeyser (1995), who said that explicit instruction indicated either that a rule was given or, as in the case of error correction, that learners were directed to attend to a specific form. Thus, Sharwood Smith's example of a technique that was -explicit, a signal when an error occurred, would be +explicit according to DeKeyser's definition if the learner knew that the signal indicated an error.

Another issue addressed by Sharwood Smith (1991) in his discussion of IE was whether the salience created is internal or external. As indicated in the quote mentioned earlier, we can see that he was discussing salience that was provided, not naturally occurring. It is well known that certain morphemes or words are naturally more salient to learners by virtue of their phonological features or position in a sentence, and these features would be examples of internally generated salience, as opposed to salience that is created through an intervention, or externally. Subsequent authors have interpreted IE as referring to externally created salience, not naturally occurring salience. What is somewhat confusing is the following quote from Sharwood Smith (1991): "The process by which language input becomes salient to the learner is termed 'input enhancement.' This process can come about as a result of deliberate manipulation, or it can be the natural outcome of some internal learning strategy" (p. 118). Despite the fact that this quote implies that IE can be a natural process, it seems clear from the rest of the article and characterizations from other authors and researchers, that it is not. Rather, IE is deliberately created salience that is intended to help the language learner.

Interestingly, however, Sharwood Smith referred in the same article to "self-generated input enhancement" (p. 129) and gave the example of a learner generating output based on learned explicit rules. Such output would then serve as a form of input for the learner, he explained. For example, a learner reads about passive sentences in a textbook. The learner then constructs a passive sentence using the learned grammar rules. The learner's language, the output, serves also as input for the learner. Again, it seems that there is no deliberate enhancement of input by the learner. Rather, Sharwood Smith seemed to be suggesting a role for output, ideas later fleshed out by Swain (1995, 2005).

Another problematic issue that needs to be raised in defining IE is what **input** is. I believe that most teachers and researchers assume input to be the available ambient speech (or writing) around a learner.

This is stated explicitly by Gass (1997), who said she preferred the term **ambient speech**, but for the sake of consistency with other literature in SLA, continued to use the term input. (Also see Williams and Fernández, this volume.) There is consensus among researchers that a learner does not take in or even attend to all available input, or ambient speech.

In his 1991 article, Sharwood Smith gave examples of negative feedback and metalinguistic rules as falling under the domain of input enhancement. Most authors classify input only as **positive evidence**, examples of what is possible in the target language. Feedback is generally considered to be **negative evidence**. The one exception to this would be recasts, which can be said to serve as both positive and negative evidence simultaneously because they are models of the correct language as well as a type of implicit correction. It is understandable perhaps that Sharwood Smith's view of input was so broad. When a learner hears a rule or receives feedback, it is available as input to the learner. Nevertheless, this is not the accepted definition of input. Furthermore, Sharwood Smith gave an example of providing learners with ungrammatical input, colored coded to show that it was ungrammatical. This too does not fit the definition of ambient speech and might even be considered a questionable teaching practice. (But see Lyster, this volume for some possible benefits.) The problem is that when Sharwood Smith used the term CR, it made sense to classify rules and feedback as CR because both rules and feedback can draw learners' attention to previously-unattended-to features and raise awareness about properties of the language. When he changed the term to IE, including negative feedback as part of the phenomenon did not make as much sense.

Despite the problems and ambiguities associated with the terms CR and IE, Sharwood Smith's coinage of IE was actually an attempt at clarification. Indeed, the term CR seems broader and vaguer than IE, and Sharwood Smith was correct to be wary of the term consciousness. It was also appropriate to place emphasis on what was happening to the input as opposed to the learner. Because one cannot be sure of what is happening in the learner's mind, one can do something to the language in an attempt to focus the learner's attention on a specific structure. Thus considering IE as an external process is the only way that makes sense. Unfortunately, the concepts did not become clearer but rather more complex because the term CR continued to be used. As mentioned earlier, Doughty and Williams (1998) classified both CR and IE as types of FonF using the Fotos and Ellis definition of CR. Doughty and

Williams defined IE as language that has been made salient by some intervention, most commonly phonological or typographical enhancement such as stress in oral language or boldface in written language. Intuitively, their definition makes sense. If we consider input as ambient language, and how it can be enhanced for the learner, both phonological and visual enhancement most immediately come to mind.

Sharwood Smith's writings (1981, 1991, 1993) were theoretical and not examples of empirical research. It is only when researchers begin to conduct studies on theories that the problems with concepts become clear. To conduct a study, terms have to be operationalized. It was probably not only the intuitive sense of what IE meant, but also an attempt to study it empirically that caused changes in the term. What follows is a chronological presentation of empirical studies that, according to the authors, examined IE. Such a presentation will help us understand the evolution of IE.

Empirical Studies of Input Enhancement

One of the first studies to examine something called input enhancement was White, Spada, Lightbown, and Ranta (1991). They defined IE as "form-focused instruction and corrective feedback" (p. 416) and examined the effect of such instruction on francophone ESL learners' formation of questions. Assessing grammatical accuracy on a variety of tasks, but not in spontaneous speech, they found a beneficial effect for their treatment.

Alanen (1995) published an empirical study of English speakers learning bound locative morphemes in semi-artificial Finnish. The title of her article, "Input enhancement and rule presentation in second language acquisition," clearly indicated that she saw IE and rule presentation as two separate techniques, unlike White et al. (1991). Alanen constructed a study consisting of a control group and three experimental groups (+enhancement, +rule presentation, +enhancement and rule presentation) and found no significant effect for the enhancement group. She operationalized enhancement as the italicization of the target morphemes in sentences that the participants read while looking at corresponding pictures they described. She referred to Sharwood Smith (1993) in passing but did not explain the term *input enhancement* explicitly. It is clear from the design of her study, however, that IE meant visual enhancements intended to make language more salient to the learner.

Jourdenais, Ota, Stauffer, Boyson, and Doughty (1995) studied textual enhancement, calling it a type of input enhancement. While it is clear that they saw textual enhancement as input enhancement, they mentioned that this technique was suggested by Sharwood Smith (1993), which it was, but only as one type of IE. In their study of enhancement of the Spanish preterit and imperfect, they found that there was a positive effect from enhancement on what was noticed by learners as well as a positive effect on the production of forms.

White (1998) looked at the effect of boldfacing pronouns and possessive determiners reasoning that such a technique would make these forms more salient to French learners of English. Her hypothesis was that the group receiving the boldfaced target structures would do better on a variety of measures. Her study, however, did not find a beneficial effect for typographical enhancement. White's reference to the technique was that it had been proposed by Sharwood Smith (1981, 1991). And again, although typographical enhancement was proposed by Sharwood Smith, it was one of many different techniques falling under the domain of what he called IE.

Leow (2001) reviewed studies of written enhancement, some of which I have discussed here. He was careful to call the phenomenon *written* input enhancement to clarify what he meant by IE. He also conducted his own study of learners of Spanish. He concluded that there were no positive effects for written enhancement and said that teachers needed to construct other tasks "that promote learners' noticing of targeted L2 forms or structures while interacting with the L2" (p. 507). He gave the example of Jourdenais et al. (1995) and Shook (1994, cited in Leow) as two of many studies that have shown a positive effect for written textual enhancement. It is interesting that Leow not only clearly defined written input enhancement, but cited Sharwood Smith in a way that did not imply that IE was equal to textual enhancement, "studies falling under the rubric of 'written input enhancement' (cf., Sharwood Smith, 1991) typically employ typographical cues—underlining, bolding, italicization, shading, different fonts or uppercase letters—to enhance saliency of targeted forms in the input" (p. 496).

Izumi (2002) examined ESL learners' use of relative clauses in a visual enhancement condition and an output condition. He too reviewed studies of visual enhancement and discussed some of the possible reasons for a lack of positive results. Nevertheless, he too found no effect for visual enhancement. He found instead that the group that was required to produce output performed better. He explained, like Sharwood Smith, that the visual enhancement was external, that is learners have their attention drawn to the feature, whereas when producing output, learners have to decide what to pay attention to themselves, and thus it was an internal attention-drawing device.

Wong (2003) also researched textual enhancement. She studied English learners reading passages that contained examples of past participle agreement in French relative clauses. She too found no effect for improved accuracy on the given structure in the enhancement group but did find that learners were better able to recall the enhanced information.

Barcroft (2003) studied English speakers learning lists of Spanish words. In addition to comparing how learners performed on enhanced and unenhanced lists, he manipulated the enhanced lists by varying the number of words that were actually visually modified. Specifically, learners studied one list in which three out of 24 words were enhanced and one in which nine out of 24 were enhanced. The hypothesis was that words would be more distinct when a smaller number were enhanced and that this would lead to stronger effects for the enhancement condition because the fewer words enhanced, the more salient they would be. His hypothesis turned out to be true and an effect for visual enhancement was found only for the group that had fewer vocabulary words in their list enhanced. Barcroft stated that IE was "the manipulation of input in a way that renders some items more perceptually salient than others" (p. 47). He did manipulate the word lists and typographically enhance some words to make them more salient, but his study is different from the others because it is the only one that examined the learning of single words provided to the learners in lists. On one hand, we might question whether or not such lists even count as input, considering the definition of input as ambient language. On the other hand, Barcroft raised an important issue, namely that salience is not an all or nothing concept and that there can be varying degrees of it. Using word lists allowed Barcroft to manipulate the degree of distinctiveness of the stimulus (the words) in his study.

Another study that is different from the previous ones was completed by Jensen and Vinther (2003), who studied repetition as a type of input enhancement. They convincingly argue that repetition can help a learner notice a feature. A learner may hear an utterance and process it for meaning and then, on the second hearing, process it for form and pay attention to the problematic structure. They claimed the learners, upon the second hearing, could direct their attention to what they wanted. So, although the learners' internal processes take over, the input to the learner was externally manipulated. They found that repetition did affect learners' scores on an imitation test with regard to three different variables: comprehension, phonological decoding, and grammatical accuracy. They also studied the effect of listening to the repeated language at different speeds but found no effect.

From the empirical research summarized above, we can see how IE has been conceived. White et al. (1991) used a broader conception of IE. Then the definition of input enhancement narrowed to refer to visual enhancement. The Jensen and Vinther study used the term to refer to repetition of items in the input. Although Jensen and Vinther completed an interesting and important study, they could have done so without calling repetition a form of IE. Perhaps they wanted to call attention to the fact that input does not have to be changed to make learners notice it, and in fact, they argue that modification inherent in interaction may sometimes be less effective than repetition for drawing learners' attention to a difficult structure. (But see Williams and Fernández, this volume for a discussion of interaction as IE.)

Other Views of Input Enhancement

Other authors in summary discussions, as opposed to empirical research, have included input enhancement as a concept in their writings. In an overview article on input and interaction, Wesche (1994) discussed input enhancement and input processing as two current (at the time) lines of research. She stated that IE was a type of pedagogical intervention in which "L2 learners' attention is directed to specific formal features of language within meaning-oriented activities with the goal of developing increased grammatical accuracy" (p. 247). She included techniques such as **input flood**, in which the frequency of a structure is increased but nothing else is done to draw the learners' attention to the structure. She, like Sharwood Smith, included feedback as a type of IE as well.

Wesche included in her review a discussion of input processing. **Input processing**, also called structured input, is a technique most often associated with VanPatten and his colleagues (e.g., VanPatten, 1996; VanPatten & Cadierno, 1993). The general principle behind input processing is that learners complete activities in which they must comprehend a certain structure to make sense of the meaning, meaning that is not available from content words alone. An example of this would be to identify a picture associated with the sentence, *The dog was chased by the cat*. The learner must understand the passive form to identify the correct picture. (See Wong, this volume for a detailed description.) In the more narrow conception of IE, input processing would not be a type of IE, and Wesche specifically separated input processing from it. In the broader conception of IE, input processing can be considered a form of IE in that the input is manipulated to force the learner to attend to certain structures. Input processing techniques usually also include explicit grammar rules presented to learners before they attend to the input.

In a theoretical article on how input can become intake by a language learner, Ying (1995) discussed both input processing instruction and input enhancement as two distinct external processes that can help learners attend to features in the input. Although he did not seem to include input processing as a type of IE, he took a broad view of IE citing the White et al. (1991) study, a study of rules and feedback that the authors called an IE study, but did not give further specific examples of IE techniques. Ying did raise an interesting point about IE regarding internal and external factors. He said that the two are not necessarily independent of one another giving the example of negotiation. He did not expand on this idea, but we can see that if a learner asks for clarification, this act is internally driven by the learner. The interlocutor can then manipulate the input to make certain problematic structures more salient by stressing them or changing their position in the sentence. So while empirical studies of IE do not mention negotiation or interaction as a type of IE, they can certainly have such an effect.

In another review article on input and intake, VanPatten (2000) classified input into four different categories (comprehensible, simplified, modified, and enhanced), the common denominator being that they are all external to the learner and not related to how the learner processes the input. He explained that the essential element of enhanced input is the attention-drawing factor. Structured input is one type of IE he said, textual enhancement is another. Because of the way the input is presented to learners in both techniques, learners are forced to pay attention to the structure in order to complete the pedagogical task.

Finally, in a recent book on input enhancement, Wong (2005) presents a very broad view of IE including chapters on input flood, textual enhancement, structured input, and grammar consciousness-raising tasks. She seemed to be returning to Sharwood Smith's original definition, that it is a deliberate attempt to make certain features more salient to the learner. In addition to visual enhancement and structured input, techniques included explicit rules or simply increasing the frequency of a structure through an input flood, similar to Jensen and Vinther's notion of repetition, where nothing is done to a structure other than repeating it. (But note Kreuz and Caucci, this volume who conclude that frequency does not imply salience.)

Conclusions and Implications for Teaching

Given the above summary of input enhancement in language teaching, it may be difficult to determine how the concept of IE informs language teaching practices. A study by Morris and Tremblay (2003) summarized the issue of varying definitions quite eloquently and perhaps can shed light on the current state of affairs in language teaching.

In a quite different type of study, Morris and Tremblay had an experimental group of French ESL learners complete a cloze dictation activity in which unstressed function words were deleted. The learners had to reconstruct the sentences with only the content words given; they had to fill in the function words themselves. Morris and Tremblay found that this task helped learners improve their grammatical accuracy. What is interesting about this study is that attention was drawn to unstressed words by *deleting* them from the written input as opposed to highlighting them. That is, learners heard complete texts, but saw only content words and had to fill in the function words themselves. In some sense, this procedure is the reverse of other studies that typographically enhance problematic structures. Using Sharwood Smith's original definition of input enhancement, this task would certainly qualify: deleting the difficult structures and forcing learners to fill in structures draws their attention to them. The interesting point about the study, however, is the following quote:

> Since the point of the experiment was to get learners to notice words that they would not normally attend to, we find ourselves at the heart of the current discussion of noticing, consciousness-raising, focus-on-form, and various other terminological avatars (Schmidt, 1990, 1993, 1995; Sharwood Smith, 1991, 1993; Harley, 1993; Doughty,

1991; Doughty and Williams, 1998; Williams, 1995; Lyster, 1994). Although the coiners of each term are unlikely to agree with us, we have chosen to group them on the basis of their common denominator: an underlying belief that second language learners can profit from having their attention called to certain language points in the acquisition process. (p. 375)

I believe that Morris and Tremblay are correct. If we define IE in the narrow sense of textual enhancement, there is only minimal evidence that it is effective. If we look at it more broadly, we can see, as they point out, that the important point is the deliberate drawing of attention to certain language features for learners. (See Leow, this volume for a comprehensive discussion of the role of attention in language learning.)

The problem is, however, that words with definitions that are extremely broad do not serve a field well. Multiple terms for the same concept do not work well either and can be confusing, particularly to those new to a field. The term *focus on form* is more commonly used than IE, and we need to distinguish the two. As stated earlier, FonF originally meant implicit feedback in the form of recasts or negotiation (Long, 1996). Doughty and Williams (1998) expanded the term as did Ellis (2001) to include not only feedback, but also proactive techniques that included explicit instruction, although still within the context of meaningful communication. In one of the few detailed discussions of FonF versus IE, Wong (2005) stated that Doughty and Williams' definition was similar to the definition of IE. Wong preferred the term IE because it emphasized the importance of input in the language learning process.

Although the use of multiple terms for similar techniques is problematic, Wong is indeed correct. Large amounts of input in the target language are a prerequisite to language learning. But that is not sufficient. The input has to be enhanced, or put another way, the learner's attention needs to be directed to features of the language through a variety of techniques, regardless of what such techniques are called.

Questions and Topics for Discussion

1) Consider how you were taught a foreign/second language. What did the instructor do to enhance the language?
2) Imagine that you are going to have students listen to a radio news story in the target language. What can you do before, during, and after the students listen to enhance the input?

3) Studies have not clearly shown a strong positive effect for textual enhancement. Why might this be so?
4) Will increasing the frequency of a structure or word in the input (input flood) increase its salience? How can this question be empirically studied?

References

Alanen, R. (1995). Input enhancement and rule presentation in second language acquisition. In R. Schmidt (Ed.), *Attention and awareness in foreign language learning* (pp. 183-216). Honolulu: University of Hawai'i Press.

Barcroft, J. (2003). Distinctiveness and bidirectional effects in input enhancement for vocabulary learning. *Applied Language Learning, 13,* 47-73.

Bialystok, E. (1981). Some evidence for the integrity and interaction of two knowledge sources. In R. Andersen (Ed.), *New dimensions in second language acquisition research* (pp. 62-74). Rowley, MA: Newbury House.

DeKeyser, R. (1995). Learning second language grammar rules: An experiment with a miniature linguistic system. *Studies in Second Language Acquisition, 17,* 379-410.

Doughty, C., & Williams, J. (1998). Pedagogical choices in focus on form. In C. Doughty & J. Williams (Eds.), *Focus on form in classroom second language acquisition* (pp. 114-138). Cambridge: Cambridge University Press.

Ellis, R. (2001). Investigating form-focused instruction. *Language Learning, 51,* Supplement, 1, 1-46.

Fotos, S. (1993). Consciousness-raising and noticing through focus on form: Grammar task performance versus formal instruction. *Applied Linguistics, 14,* 385-407.

Fotos, S., & Ellis, R. (1991). Communicating about grammar: A task-based approach. *TESOL Quarterly, 25,* 605-628.

Gass, S. (1997). *Input, interaction, and the second language learner.* Mahwah, NJ: Erlbaum.

Izumi, S. (2002). Output, input enhancement, and the noticing hypothesis: An experimental study on ESL relativization. *Studies in Second Language Acquisition, 24,* 541-577.

Jensen, E., & Vinther, T. (2003). Exact repetition as input enhancement in second language acquisition. *Language Learning, 53,* 373-428.

Jourdenais, R., Ota, M., Stauffer, S., Boyson, B., & Doughty, C. (1995). Does textual enhancement promote noticing? A think-aloud protocol analysis. In R. Schmidt (Ed.), *Attention and awareness in foreign language learning* (pp. 183-216). Honolulu: University of Hawai'i Press.

Krashen, S. (1981). *Second language acquisition and second language learning.* London: Pergamon.

Krashen, S. (1982). *Principles and practice in second language acquisition.* London: Pergamon.

Krashen, S., & Terrell, T. (1983). *The natural approach: Language acquisition in the classroom.* Oxford: Pergamon/Alemany.

Larsen-Freeman, D., & Long, M. (1991). *An introduction to second language acquisition research.* London: Longman.

Leow, R. (2001). Do learners notice enhanced forms while interacting with the L2 input? An online and offline study of the role of written input enhancement in L2 reading. *Hispania, 84,* 496-509.

Long, M. (1981). Input, interaction and second language acquisition. In H. Winitz (Ed.), *Native language and foreign language acquisition* (pp. 259-278). New York: Annals of the New York Academy of Sciences.

Long, M. (1983). Linguistic and conversational adjustments to non-native speakers. *Studies in Second Language Acquisition, 5,* 177-193.

Long, M. (1996). The role of the linguistic environment in second language acquisition. In W. Ritchie & T. Bhatia (Eds.), *Handbook of language acquisition. Vol. 2: Second language acquisition* (pp. 413-468). San Diego: Academic.

Long, M. (2000). Focus on form in task-based language teaching. In R.D. Lambert & E. Shohamy (Eds.), *Language policy and pedagogy (*pp. 179-192). Philadephia: John Benjamins.

Long, M., & Crookes, G. (1992). Three approaches to task-based syllabus design. *TESOL Quarterly, 26,* 27-56.

McLaughlin, B. (1978). The monitor model: Some methodological considerations. *Language Learning, 28,* 309-332.

Morris, L., & Tremblay, M. (2003). The impact of attending to unstressed words on the acquisition of written grammatical morphology by French-speaking ESL students. *Canadian Modern Language Review, 58,* 364-385.

Norris, J., & Ortega, L. (2000). Effectiveness of L2 instruction: A research synthesis and quantitative meta-analysis. *Language Learning, 50,* 441-528.

Sharwood Smith, M. (1981). Consciousness-raising and the second language learner. *Applied Linguistics, 2,* 159-168.

Sharwood Smith, M. (1991). Speaking to many minds: On the relevance of different types of language information for the L2 learner. *Second Language Research, 17,* 118-136.

Sharwood Smith, M. (1993). Input enhancement in structured SLA: Theoretical bases. *Studies in Second Language Acquisition, 15,* 165-179.

Swain, M. (1985). Communicative competence: Some roles of comprehensible input and comprehensible output in its development. In S. Gass & C. Madden (Eds.), *Input and second language acquisition* (pp. 235-256). Rowley, MA: Newbury House.

Swain, M. (1995). Three functions of output in second language learning. In G. Cook & B. Seidlhofer (Eds.), *Principle and practice in applied linguistics* (pp. 125-144). Oxford: Oxford University Press.

Swain, M. (2005) The output hypothesis: Theory and research. In E. Hinkel (Ed.), *Handbook of research in second language teaching and learning* (pp. 471-484). Mahwah, NJ: Erlbaum.

VanPatten, B. (1996). *Input processing and grammar instruction.* Norwood, NJ: Ablex.

VanPatten, B. (2000). Thirty years of input (or intake, the neglected sibling). In B. Swierzbin, F. Morris, M. Anderson, C. Klee, & E. Tarone (Eds.), *Social and cognitive factors in second language acquisition* (pp. 287-311). Somerville, MA: Cascadilla Press.

VanPatten, B., & Cadierno, T. (1993). Explicit instruction and input processing. *Studies in Second Language Acquisition, 15,* 225-243.

Wesche, M. (1994). Input and interaction in second language acquisition. In C. Gallaway & B. Richard (Eds.), *Input and interaction in language acquisition* (pp. 219-249). Cambridge: Cambridge University Press.

White, J. (1998). Getting the learners' attention: A typographical input enhancement study. In C. Doughty & J. Williams (Eds.), *Focus on form in classroom second language acquisition* (pp. 85-113). Cambridge: Cambridge University Press.

White, L., Spada, N., Lightbown, P., & Ranta, L. (1991). Input enhancement and L2 question formation. *Applied Linguistics, 4,* 416-432.

Williams, J. (2005). Form-focused instruction. In E. Hinkel (Ed.), *Handbook of research in second language teaching and learning* (pp. 671-692). Mahwah, NJ: Erlbaum.

Wong, W. (2003). The effects of textual enhancement and simplified input on L2 comprehension and acquisition of non-meaningful grammatical form. *Applied Language Learning, 14,* 109-132.

Wong, W. (2005). *Input enhancement: From theory and research to the classroom.* NewYork: McGraw Hill.

Ying, H. (1995). What sort of input is needed for intake? *International Review of Applied Linguistics, 33,* 175-194.

Chapter 2
Salience as a Concept in Cognitive Psychology

Roger J. Kreuz & Gina M. Caucci, University of Memphis

The concept of salience is a pervasive construct within the field of psychology: it influences affect, behavior, and the workings of the cognitive system. With regard to cognition, salience plays an important role in perception, attention, memory, and language. Even though it is a central part of psychological theory and practice, some of its effects are poorly understood, while others are paradoxical. This chapter will provide an overview of salience in cognition, and review some of the lines of research where it has assumed a prominent role.

Definitions of salience tend to be unsatisfying because they must be written so broadly. One influential dictionary of psychology describes salience as "Distinctiveness, prominence, [or] obviousness. The term is widely used in the study of perception and cognition to refer to any aspect of a stimulus that, for any of many reasons, stands out from the rest" (Reber & Reber, 2001, p. 220). The authors add that salience "may be the result of emotional, motivational or cognitive factors and is not necessarily associated with physical factors such as intensity, clarity, or size" (p. 220). This claim highlights the inherently psychological nature of the concept: it is not possible, a priori, to predict which stimuli in the environment will recruit one's attention, or stamp themselves on one's memory. However, by exploring what salience is, and what salience is not, we will arrive at a better understanding of the internal processes that underlie both thought and action.

What Salience is Not: Frequency and Familiarity

What does a penny look like? Would you recognize one if you saw it? Most people would consider such questions to be almost insulting: we know what coins look like because we handle them on a daily basis, and they are extremely familiar to us. However, we should not make the mistake of equating familiarity with memory. For it turns out that even the most familiar of stimuli may not, in fact, have made much of an impression on the cognitive system.

Let's prove the point. Which features appear on the front of a penny besides Lincoln's profile? Does his head face to the left or to the right? You may feel certain that the date is present, but how about the words "one cent," "Liberty," or "In God we trust"? How about "United States of America" or "E pluribus unum"? Suddenly, you may not be so certain. Nickerson and Adams (1979) asked subjects to draw the head side of the one cent coin, and found that their respondents performed remarkably poorly. On average, the subjects got only three of eight features correct. This study, and others like it, suggest that we fail to attend to many of the elements in our environment, and as a result, our recall memory for them will be quite poor.

We can see the same phenomenon in the domain of second language acquisition (SLA) with regard to the learning of grammatical gender. Even though nouns appear with their appropriate articles over and over again, students may fail to encode these forms (Harley, 1998), just as we fail to encode the details on the front of a penny. As Schmidt (1994) has pointed out, attention is required to notice and register the invariances in our environment. Therefore, salient stimuli are not the same as frequent or familiar stimuli, and attention is the crucial mediator between the world and long-term memory.

In fact, we may actually attend to only a small fraction of the world around us. Classic theories of attention (e.g., Broadbent, 1958) assume that the sensory world is too rich to allow for a complete analysis of everything we see, hear, touch, and taste. Instead, attention might be best thought of as a spotlight that plays over the stage of our lives, leaving most of the perceptual world in darkness.

This idea is common in discussions of "mindfulness" and "mindlessness" (e.g., Langer, 1990). We conserve our cognitive resources by going about many of our daily affairs, such as driving, as if we were on autopilot. It is only when we must react to some new stimulus (e.g., a disabled car in the passing lane) that the task before us recruits our cognitive resources. It seems clear, therefore, that any discussion of salience must focus critically on perception and attention.

Salience and Attention

Even very simple forms of life will react to novel elements in their environment. Since the detection of salient stimuli is highly adaptive, we can assume that there are strong evolutionary pressures on species, and therefore individuals, to pay attention to potential dangers and opportunities. Associations between stimuli, such as those required for classical conditioning, are learned more quickly when the stimuli are distinctive in some way. In addition, if two stimuli, such as a bright light and a dim light, *both* predict a reinforcer, the conditioned response will be stronger to the bright light than to the dim one. This phenomenon, called **overshadowing**, is not predicted solely by the physical intensity of the stimulus, but rather by a subjective experience on the part of the learner (Schwartz & Reisberg, 1991).

The perceptual basis of attention is clearly seen in the Gestalt principles of organization (Wertheimer, 1923). The claim is that we perceive objects as unified wholes rather than as collections of unrelated elements. For example, Wertheimer's principle of **proximity** states that objects that are close together are perceived as belonging together. The principle of **similarity** purports that similar elements are perceived as belonging together. This implies that stimuli that are not near and/or similar to each other should recruit attention (and possess salience), because they will stand out as not belonging to a perceptual whole.

A modern account of such effects can be found in the feature-integration theory of Anne Treisman (Treisman & Gelade, 1980; Treisman, 1993). Her account of attention and perceptual processing involves two kinds of attentional processes. In **distributed attention**, we process all parts of a scene at once, via parallel processing. This is a relatively automatic, effortless process. In contrast, **focused attention** is the processing of objects one-by-one. Such serial searching is more demanding of resources from the cognitive system.

Imagine, for example, that you are searching for a red pen in a drawer full of blue pens. The red pen will "pop out" of its surroundings because the sought-after object differs from the others according to one simple feature: that of color. Such quick searches on the basis of one particular feature are the province of distributed attention. Now, however, imagine that you are searching for your favorite blue pen in a drawer full of other blue pens. In this case, you must focus your attention on each object, considering each pen in turn. A serial search using focused attention would naturally be more time-consuming.

It should be kept in mind, however, that these attentional processes are affected by the subjective aspects of the scene. For example, there are few stimuli more salient than one's own name, which will pop out of a list appearing in a newspaper, or be heard even in the middle of a crowded, noisy environment—the so-called "cocktail party effect" (Moray, 1959).

Salience and Memory

So far, we have addressed issues of salience and how they relate to attention and perception. Now we turn to perhaps a more relevant question: what, if any, are the effects of salience on memory? In general, salient items "stand out" from their surroundings, and have a facilitative effect on memory. This may seem fairly intuitive. Think about viewing a list of vocabulary items where one of the words has been written in a different color ink. That item would most likely stand out, drawing your attention in turn. If you are asked later to recall some of the words appearing on the list, you would perform above chance in recalling the disparate item.

One line of research has attempted to discern the processes involved in memory for salient items or events. A good example of this phenomenon is the **von Restorff** (or isolation) **effect**, which is defined as "the enhancement of memory for events that differ, or deviate from their context" (Kelley & Nairne, 2001, p. 54). A similar issue was addressed earlier in the discussion of pop-out effects. In both cases, the anomalous or distinct items have an attention-grabbing effect that tends to facilitate our cognitive processes and make the items easier to attend to and remember.

In most experiments aimed at testing the von Restorff effect, participants are shown lists of items wherein one item is made distinct from the other items by changing it physically (e.g., size, color, or font) or semantically (e.g., the word *banana* in a list of animal names). Cimbalo, Capria, Neider, and Wilkins (1977) reported that the manipulations that most successfully isolate an item are size, color, and spacing. When participants are later tested on their memory for such distinctive items in a list, they show significantly higher levels of recall. Kelley and Nairne's participants (2001, experiment 2) demonstrated superior recall for isolated items both when they were printed at twice the size of the control items (large isolate condition) and when they were half the size of the control items (small isolate condition). The researchers believe that these results are important because it could otherwise be debated whether the superior recall in the large isolate condition was due simply to perceptual salience (Kelley & Nairne, 2001). By showing this effect with the small isolate condition, they demonstrate that what is important is the *relative* difference, and not the fact that some of the words were larger than others (Kelley & Nairne, 2001). The isolation effect has implications for students learning a second language. By changing the size or color of the font of important vocabulary items or grammar rules in a list, for example, students will be more likely to remember the manipulated items (Cimbalo, Capria, Neider, & Wilkins, 1977).

One theory that has been offered to account for the superior recall of distinctive items is Craik and Lockhart's levels of processing framework (Craik & Lockhart, 1972). They speculate that the anomalous items are processed at a deeper level, which causes people to think more about their meaning rather than just their superficial characteristics, such as a word printed in capital letters.

Script Violations

Unfortunately, within any line of research there is usually evidence that can be found to contradict it. For the von Restorff effect, that evidence is called a **script violation**. A script refers to our general knowledge and comprehension of entire events or episodes (Bartlett, 1932/1995). As stated earlier, the salience of an item or event is not tied to that item itself. In fact, there may be any number of reasons why people misremember an item or event.

One of the most well known examples of a script is the restaurant script (Schank & Abelson, 1977). We possess knowledge of what takes place when someone goes to a restaurant, and in what order these events occur (e.g., first they sit down, then they order food, eat the food, and then pay the bill). A prediction that follows from this is that if you forgot to pay the bill, you might mistakenly believe that you had, because that action is an important part of the script. This is a case where a distinctive event has gone unnoticed, because its nonoccurrence violates our knowledge of what takes place when someone goes to a restaurant. With regard to SLA, one way to get around this problem of distinctive events going unnoticed would be to inform students that distinctive items are important and should be given special attention.

Implicit Versus Explicit Memory

We now turn to two types of memory that have been a focus of research in cognitive psychology, as well as widely discussed in the SLA literature: implicit and explicit memory. Ellis (1993) notes that differences in SLA instruction are based on either implicit, automatic processing, or explicit rule-based processing. The prevailing view at different points in time tends to influence which of these methods dominates in the field of second language instruction (Ellis, 1993).

Many studies have been conducted to determine which of these two instructional approaches is superior. DeKeyser (1998) reports evidence that suggests that implicit instruction leads to better learning than explicit instruction. However, students may be better at *noticing* when something is correct versus incorrect, but not able to give a reason *why* it is correct. In other words, they haven't acquired the rules, but instead seem to be making judgments based on how similar an item is to an exemplar they were exposed to previously. In their review of the literature on second language instruction, Norris and Ortega (2000) suggest a different focus. They point out that the emphasis should not be on which is better (implicit or explicit knowledge), but rather that there are problems with the methodologies being utilized in these research studies and the way these constructs are being operationalized. For example, there is a tendency for researchers to use explicit memory tasks (e.g., asking participants to report what they remember) even when the interest is in studying implicit memory.

In cognitive psychology, evidence has been found to support the importance of implicit memory. Within the field, there have been many studies of a phenomenon called **repetition priming**. Repetition priming occurs when a word has repeatedly appeared within a body of text, and then is remembered better than words that were not repeated. An important point is that people may not even be aware that they were being primed by the word, or that they had even seen the word more than once. Nevertheless, we would implicitly demonstrate better memory for that word. One of the most commonly used implicit memory tasks is the word-stem completion task. For example, if, after reading this section on implicit and explicit memory, you were given the stem IMP _ _ _ _ _, you would be more likely to complete the stem with *implicit* than with *imposter*. These results could occur even if the repeated word had not been a major focus of the narrative.

Repetition priming should not be taken as evidence that explicit memory is insignificant, however. For example, learning a skill is an example of an explicitly taught rule. Over time, that skill becomes more automatic with practice. In other words, knowledge of the skill leads to using it in a more straightforward way without having to refer back to prior knowledge (DeKeyser, 1998). There is no reason to think that second language acquisition could not be contained under the umbrella of such skills. Therefore, over time and with explicitly based rule knowledge, speaking and comprehending the second language will become easier and more automatic.

Jacoby and Dallas (1981) studied implicit and explicit memory by utilizing the Craik and Lockhart (1972) levels of processing paradigm. Participants were given a list of words and asked questions about each word. These questions ranged from queries about the physical characteristics of the word, which required only shallow processing, to their semantic features, which required deep processing. Subsequently, participants were given two memory tasks: an explicit recognition task and an implicit word presentation task. For the recognition task, the words that were processed more deeply were remembered 95% of the time, in comparison to only 51% for those words that were processed at a shallow level. For the implicit memory task, words were presented to the participants on a computer screen for 35 milliseconds (a second contains 1,000 milliseconds). For the previously processed words, recognition was 80%, regardless of the level at which they were processed. In contrast, those words that had not been in the original list were recognized only 60% of the time.

There has been a debate about the importance of implicit versus explicit knowledge in SLA, with Ellis (1993) observing that there is a need for further research on the function that these two forms of knowledge play in SLA. In one of his studies, participants were assigned to a random group (implicit), a rule group (explicit), or a rule and instances group (implicit and explicit) in order to learn one feature of written Welsh, the soft mutation. His results suggest that there is a preference for the combination of implicit exposure and the demonstration of explicit rules with clarifying examples (Ellis, 1993). These results relate to the earlier discussion of salience and distinctiveness. By exposing the learner to the second language, the subconscious acquisition of the language is facilitated, but it seems necessary to bolster this method with an explicit explanation of the language's rules to allow learners to monitor their output (Krashen, 1982, 1985; as cited in Ellis, 1993).

The Zeigarnik Effect

If you are the sort of person who keeps "to do" lists, do you find it easier to remember items that you haven't yet completed, or the items that you've already crossed off your list? Most people report that tasks not yet completed seem more salient, and this turns out to affect their memorability. A Russian-born psychologist, Bliuma Zeigarnik, became intrigued by this phenomenon when she asked a waiter in a Berlin café to provide a receipt for her party after having paid the bill. The waiter, who had given perfect service without the benefit of a paper record, protested that he could no longer remember the order because it had already been paid for (Thorne & Henley, 2005). Zeigarnik (1927) experimentally verified this phenomenon by giving tasks to participants and allowing them to complete some tasks but not others. Just as predicted, the participants' recall of the uncompleted tasks was better than for the tasks that they had, in fact, completed. Seen from this perspective, salience is tied to prospective memory, with completed tasks rapidly diminishing in salience.

Salience and Language

For many years, researchers in psycholinguistics assumed that the exact words used by speakers or writers (the surface form) were "thrown away" by the hearer or reader, leaving behind only the gist meaning of utterances and sentences (e.g., Sachs, 1967). One problem with this view is that there seems to be a large number of exceptions. Think back, for example, to the last time someone insulted you. Chances are, you remember the exact words that the speaker employed. If you later recounted the episode to a sympathetic audience, you probably had no difficulty in relating the specific epithet that was used. It seems unlikely that you would say, "John insulted me, although I don't really remember what he said." Not surprisingly, therefore, researchers have found that, at least in some circumstances, the surface form of statements is remembered by their addressees. Ultimately, this research suggests that statements that are salient to the individual tend to be remembered in their verbatim form.

Keenan, MacWhinney, and Mayhew (1977) proposed that statements that are high in **interactional content** should be well remembered. These researchers defined interactional content as the "speaker's intentions, beliefs, and attitudes toward the listener" (p. 549). To test their hypothesis, they recorded and transcribed statements made during a luncheon discussion group. Thirty hours after this luncheon, participants were presented with statements that had been expressed verbatim during the discussion, as well as statements that were paraphrases of the originals. Their task was to choose which sentence had actually been spoken.

A statement with high interactional content actually uttered at the meeting was "Italians, you know what Italians are like, they had a strike, they had a heat wave" (p. 552). The participants had to choose between this sentence and another that preserved the meaning, but which differed in its surface form: "Everyone knows what happens in Italy, first they had a strike, then they had a heat wave" (p. 552). In contrast, a sentence with low interactional content was "You put a little morpheme that says you're going to choose the Object as Subject" (p. 552). Once again, participants had to choose between the original and one that differed in its surface form. The results revealed the importance of interactional content: statements with high interactional content resulted in very good memory for the surface form, whereas participants were unable to differentiate between the original and a paraphrase for statements low in interactional content.

The results of this study were echoed in the work of Kintsch and Bates (1977), who looked at memory for statements delivered in a classroom lecture. Three types of sentences were examined: topic statements, details, and extraneous statements, such as jokes and announcements. They also looked at recognition memory over a longer period of time than in the Keenan et al. research. Two days after the lecture, participants were able to pick out the verbatim forms of all three sentence types. After five days, however, the participants were accurate in picking out the verbatim forms only for the extraneous remarks. Although these results may be somewhat depressing for those in the teaching profession, they underscore the importance of distinctiveness and the role that it plays in the memory process. Just as with the von Restorff effect discussed in the previous section, it appears that information that differs from its surrounding context will be processed in a way that will allow greater recognition on a later occasion.

This line of research is echoed by work on a phenomenon called the **self-reference effect**. This refers to superior memory for information that has been encoded in relation to oneself. For example, imagine that you are being shown a list of trait adjectives. After each item, you are asked to think about it in relation to yourself, or in relation to some well-known other person, such as David Letterman. If you are asked to think about the concept "greedy" in relation to yourself, for example, you can probably *think* of specific examples or counterexamples of this trait in your behavior (e.g., "Gee, I did take the last slice of pizza last night without asking anyone else if they wanted it"). However, if you are asked to think about a trait like "impulsive" with regard to David Letterman, you will probably be able to form only a general impression of whether or not Letterman exemplifies this trait.

The consequences of such manipulations are clear: information that has been related to the self shows a consistent advantage in later memory for that material (Symons & Johnson, 1997). This self-reference advantage also seems to emerge relatively early, with children as young as five years demonstrating the effect (Sui & Zhu, 2005). It may be the case that such information is being encoded more deeply, or that it is being considered in connection with the most salient of psychological constructs: the self. The self concept is both highly organized and frequently used, and these characteristics seem to confer strong mnemonic advantages on anything that is related to it.

Individual Differences

One criticism of research in cognitive psychology has been the lack of attention paid to individual differences. More often than not, researchers in this field ignore these differences and work under the assumption that cognitive processes operate identically across all people. However, there are two areas in which individual differences have received empirical attention: the role of expertise, and the importance of schemata.

Imagine, for example, that you are an expert mechanic. Someone brings their car to you because they cannot figure out what is wrong with it. When you open the hood and look inside, you are able to identify the problem right away. This is because, as an expert, you understand how engines work and how they are supposed to function. Perhaps you have seen other cars with similar problems many times before. In other words, you have the ability to look at the engine and make sense of it. Certain features of the engine will be more salient to you than they are to a novice mechanic. Furthermore, people who possess expertise in certain domains tend to view different items as salient in comparison to novices.

A **schema** is the term used to refer to individual frameworks and knowledge structures in long-term memory. In other words, our life experiences and our general world knowledge of events and concepts will shape the way we process the environment. Consequently, what we remember from a news story about the President will be affected by what we already know about him, as well as our political beliefs and the opinions of other people we know. For example, someone with opposing views might be more inclined to forget a positive aspect of a story regarding the President, while at the same time remembering and even exaggerating the negative aspects. (For an example of such memory distortions, see Sulin & Dooling, 1974.)

In the definition of salience given at the beginning of this chapter, we introduced the idea that an item's salience is not necessarily tied to the item itself. Much of what we find to be salient will be determined by our individual cognitive processes and experiences. Within the SLA research literature, there has been much attention paid to differences in the individual learner. Two examples of such individual differences are learner readiness and developmental readiness. Park (2004) notes the importance of understanding and being cognizant of a learner's willingness and ability to take in presented material. In other words, if the student is ill-equipped to attend to the material, there will be no further processing of that material. Park believes that there must be a match between the learner's "internal syllabus" and the teacher's plan for the course in order for acquisition to take place (Park, 2004, p. 5).

There have been other discussions about the importance of learner readiness and SLA. For example, Sharwood Smith (1991) makes the argument that the learner will not necessarily recognize what the instructor is attempting to salient. In other words, he notes the problem is in assuming that the teacher's notion of salience and the learner's notion of salience correspond. One problem with the concept of internal salience is that it is difficult if not impossible to empirically investigate. Furthermore, this assumes that the learner is even aware of what he or she deems more salient. As discussed previously, much of our cognitive processing, including attention and memory, occurs implicitly.

One suggestion might be to talk to students about their interests and hobbies. As Park (2004) explains, one student might find vocabulary words pertaining to cooking more salient and attend to them, while another student might find the culture surrounding a foreign language to be interesting and consequently find vocabulary or narratives regarding the culture as more salient. It might be important for instructors to take this individualistic approach in order to strike a balance between what the syllabus deems important and what the learner observes as salient. Long and Robinson (1998) suggest that an analysis of students' needs be conducted before the initiation of an instructor's lessons.

The age of the learner also plays a major role in SLA. Some concepts may be too advanced, and certain features may need to be presented as more salient to a younger group of learners compared to a class of adult students. For example, children who have not yet mastered the grammar forms of their first language may not yet be ready to focus on those of a second language. Therefore, instructors should keep in mind the developmental readiness of the learner.

How Can Salience be Measured?

Researchers interested in salience have traditionally studied it by using fairly indirect behavioral techniques of the type that have been reviewed in the preceding sections, such as its effects on conditioning, attention, and memory. However, recent technological advances have made it possible to study salience effects in a much more direct way. We will consider two such techniques: eye movements and event-related potentials (ERPs).

Eye Movements

A great deal of the cerebral cortex is devoted to the processing of visual information, and it seems fair to say that we are, as a species, visually oriented. As a result, the study of eye movements and fixation (gaze) duration promises to provide a much more fine-grained analysis of how we inspect the salient features of our environment.

Although eye tracking can be accomplished in a variety of ways, the primary methodology involves the measurement of infrared light as it is reflected by the cornea of a participant. These reflections can be captured by a camera and recorded by a computer, which can correlate the reflections with the information being presented, such as lines of text (Just & Carpenter, 1987). Although the details of these methodologies are not relevant to the present discussion, it is worth noting that such techniques are not without their problems: head movements and calibration procedures can be problematic, and the wearing of contact lenses or bifocals by participants also presents difficulties. Nonetheless, eye tracking provides an unprecedented moment-by-moment glimpse into the realm of visual cognition.

The results from a representative study (Just & Carpenter, 1980) indicate that readers do not fixate on every word within a line of text. Instead, only about 80% of content words (such as nouns, verbs, adjectives, and adverbs) are fixated, compared to 40% of function words (such as articles, conjunctions, and prepositions). Words that the text signals as important receive longer fixations, as well as words that are low in frequency. Eye tracking has also been used to study other visual tasks like music reading and facial recognition (for a review, see Rayner, 1998). Although the results of such studies have been interpreted in a variety of ways, one conclusion is that salient stimuli will receive more and longer fixations than information that is less important.

Event-Related Potentials

As we have seen in previous sections, individuals are attuned to the stimuli in their environment that are distinctive or unusual. The registration of such stimuli can be directly studied by observing changes in electrical activity in the cortex.

It had long been assumed that such changes could not be correlated with particular mental events. When a participant's response to a particular external event is measured using an electroencephalogram (EEG), the resulting pattern represents a myriad of ongoing brain processes, and appears to be uninterpretable. An analogy may make this clearer. Imagine that you are standing outside of a baseball stadium while a game is being played. You can hear the roar of the crowd, which is made up of many individual voices, and there may be an occasional swell of excitement when something important happens. However, you would be hard pressed to figure out the exact score based on this sort of input.

Researchers have solved this problem by making recordings from discrete locations on the scalp, and by averaging the data from dozens or even hundreds of stimulus presentations. When the data are averaged in this way, the random fluctuations in activity are smoothed out, leaving behind characteristic changes in amplitude that seem to be associated with particular cognitive operations.

One such change in amplitude is referred to as P300, or simply P3. This refers to a positive voltage displacement occurring about 300 milliseconds after the presentation of a particular stimulus (Squires, Squires, & Hillyard, 1975). The P300 component is elicited by the presentation of low-frequency stimuli in the context of other stimuli that occur more frequently. So it is possible to study how an individual responds to distinctive, salient, or unusual stimuli at the level of electrical activity in the brain, and to map out the time course of such processing in a precise way.

Conclusions

It should be clear from this review that salience is a central concept in the field of cognition, and we have described its effects in a variety of contexts. At the same time, we have shown that what *is* salient will vary from person to person, and from situation to situation. Therefore, to capitalize on the benefits of salience, one must have knowledge of the individual and his or her context. An awareness of salience can confer tangible pedagogical benefits, but it should be clear that one size will not fit all. In addition, as researchers identify new ways to study salience, it should become possible to specify more precisely how people attend to and respond to salient stimuli in their environment, including the second language classroom.

Questions and Topics for Discussion

1) How does implicit memory differ from explicit memory? Provide an example of each form of memory.
2) Why should familiarity not be equated with salience? Try to think of a familiar object that most people would have difficulty describing.
3) Imagine a schema for a familiar event or activity, and try to specify the components of that schema. Do you think that someone else would provide the same set of components, or would there be important differences across people?
4) According to the self-reference effect, what would be a helpful strategy for learning foreign language vocabulary?
5) How could the von Restorff (isolation) effect be used to facilitate classroom instruction of second-language vocabulary?

Notes

Support for the preparation of this chapter was provided by a Center of Excellence Grant from the State of Tennessee to the Department of Psychology at the University of Memphis. The authors would like to thank Allison Fusini for comments on an earlier version of this chapter.

References

Bartlett, F.C. (1932/1995). *Remembering: A study in experimental and social psychology*. Cambridge: Cambridge University Press.

Broadbent, D.E. (1958). *Perception and communication*. New York: Pergamon.

Cimbalo, R.S., Capria, R.A., Neider, L.L., & Wilkins, M.C. (1977). Isolation effect: Overall lost facilitation in short-term memory. *Acta Psychologica, 41*, 419-432.

Craik, F.I.M., & Lockhart, R.S. (1972). Levels of processing: A framework for memory research. *Journal of Verbal Learning and Verbal Behavior, 11*, 671-684.

DeKeyser, R.M. (1998). Beyond focus on form: Cognitive perspectives on learning and practicing second language grammar. In C. Doughty & J. Williams (Eds.), *Focus on form in classroom second language acquisition* (pp. 42-63). Cambridge: Cambridge University Press.

Ellis, N. (1993). Rules and interactions in foreign language learning: Interactions of explicit and implicit knowledge. *European Journal of Cognitive Psychology, 5*, 289-318.

Harley, B. (1998). The role of focus-on-form tasks in promoting child L2 acquisition. In C. Doughty & J. Williams (Eds.), *Focus on form in classroom second language acquisition* (pp.156-174). Cambridge: Cambridge University Press.

Jacoby, L.L., & Dallas, M. (1981). On the relationship between autobiographical memory and perceptual learning. *Journal of Experimental Psychology: General, 110*, 306-340.

Just, M.A., & Carpenter, P.A. (1980). A theory of reading: From eye fixations to comprehension. *Psychological Review, 87*, 329-354.

Just, M.A., & Carpenter, P.A. (1987). *The psychology of reading and language comprehension*. Boston: Allyn & Bacon, Inc.

Keenan, J.M., MacWhinney, B., & Mayhew, D. (1977). Pragmatics in memory: A study of natural conversation. *Journal of Verbal Learning and Verbal Behavior, 16*, 549-560.

Kelley, M.R., & Nairne, J.S. (2001). von Restorff revisited: Isolation, generation, and memory for order. *Journal of Experimental Psychology: Learning, Memory and Cognition, 27*, 54-66.

Kintsch, W., & Bates, E. (1977). Recognition memory for statements from a classroom lecture. *Journal of Experimental Psychology: Human Learning and Memory, 3*, 150-159.

Langer, E.J. (1990). *Mindfulness*. New York: Addison Wesley.

Long, M.H., & Robinson, P. (1998). Focus on form: Theory, research, and practice. In C. Doughty & J. Williams (Eds.), *Focus on form in classroom second language acquisition* (pp. 15-41). Cambridge: Cambridge University Press.

Moray, N. (1959). Attention in dichotic listening: Affective cues and the influence of instructions. *Quarterly Journal of Experimental Psychology, 11*, 56-60.

Nickerson, R.S., & Adams, M.J. (1979). Long-term memory for a common object. *Cognitive Psychology, 11*, 287-307.

Norris, J.M., & Ortega, L. (2000). Effectiveness of L2 instruction: A research synthesis and quantitative meta-analysis. *Language Learning, 50*, 441-528.

Park, E.S. (2004). Constraints of implicit focus on form: Insights from a study of input enhancement. *Working Papers in TESOL and Applied Linguistics, 4*, 1-30.

Rayner, K. (1998). Eye movements in reading and information processing: 20 years of research. *Psychological Bulletin 124*, 372-422.

Reber, A.S., & Reber, A. (2001). *The penguin dictionary of psychology, third edition*. London: Penguin Books, Ltd.

Sachs, J. (1967). Recognition memory for syntactic and semantic aspects of connected discourse. *Perception and Psychophysics, 2*, 437-442.

Schank, R.C., & Abelson, R.P. (1977). *Scripts, plans, goals, and understanding*. Hillsdale, NJ: Lawrence Erlbaum.

Schmidt, R. (1994). Implicit learning and the cognitive unconscious: Of artificial grammars and SLA. In N. Ellis (Ed.), *Implicit and explicit learning of languages* (pp. 165-209). London: Academic Press.

Schwartz, B., & Reisberg, D. (1991). *Learning and memory*. New York: W.W. Norton.

Sharwood Smith, M. (1991). Consciousness-raising and the second language learner. *Applied Linguistics, 11*, 159-168.

Squires, K.C., Squires, N.K., & Hillyard, S.A. (1975). Decision-related cortical potentials during an auditory signal detection task with cued observation intervals. *Journal of Experimental Psychology: Human Perception and Performance, 1*, 268-279.

Sui, J., & Zhu, Y. (2005). Five-year-olds can show the self-reference advantage. *International Journal of Behavioral Development, 29*, 382-387.

Sulin, R.A., & Dooling, D.J. (1974). Intrusions of a thematic idea in retention of prose. *Journal of Experimental Psychology, 103*, 255-262.

Symons, C.S., & Johnson, B.T. (1997). The self-reference effect in memory: A meta-analysis. *Psychological Bulletin, 121*, 371-394.

Thorne, B.M., & Henley, T.B. (2005). *Connections in the history and systems of psychology, third edition.* New York: Houghton Mifflin.

Treisman, A. (1993). The perception of features and objects. In A. Baddeley & L. Weiskrantz (Eds.), *Attention: Selection, awareness, and control* (pp. 5-35). Oxford: Clarendon.

Treisman, A., & Gelade, G. (1980). A feature-integration theory of attention. *Cognitive Psychology, 12*, 97-136.

Wertheimer, M. (1923). Untersuchungen zur Lehre von der Gestalt. II. *Psychologische Forschung, 4*, 301-350.

Zeigarnik, B. (1927). Über Behalten von erledigten und unerledigten Handlungen [On the retention of finished and unfinished acts]. *Psychologische Forschung, 9*, 1-85.

Chapter 3
Input Enhancement in Classroom-Based SLA Research: An Attentional Perspective

Ronald P. Leow, Georgetown University

The notion of input enhancement has permeated several distinct strands of research in pedagogical second language acquisition (SLA) literature (e.g., processing instruction, consciousness-raising, input flooding, focus on form, textual enhancement, oral interaction). This chapter seeks to address the theoretical, empirical, and methodological issues surrounding this notion by tracing the original theoretical underpinning of the term "input enhancement," namely, the role of consciousness or awareness in "learner knowledge" and "learner behavior," and situating this underpinning within current theoretical attentional frameworks. To this end, the chapter (1) reports on current approaches to the roles of attention and awareness in SLA, (2) attempts to situate input enhancement within an attentional framework by discussing how the current theoretical underpinnings have evolved from Sharwood Smith's initial notion of language consciousness-raising from both an attention and an awareness perspective, and (3) based on the above, provides a methodological critique of current empirical research on the effects of enhanced input on comprehension and second language development.

Rationale for Situating Input Enhancement within an Attentional Framework

The term "input enhancement" was first coined by Sharwood Smith (1991, 1993) to override his previous term "language consciousness-raising" (Sharwood Smith, 1981), that is, the guidance teachers provide for promoting second/foreign language (L2) learners' self discovery or conscious awareness of the formal features of the L2. According to Sharwood Smith, input enhancement can be defined from two perspectives: an external perspective, which is any pedagogical attempt (usually by a teacher) to make more salient specific features of L2 input in an effort to draw learners' attention to such enhanced features and an internal perspective, that is, it is the learners' internal mechanism that makes salient specific features in the input. The major theoretical underpinning of either perspective is, without doubt, that learners need to pay attention to specific items in the input before such information can be taken in with the potential of being processed further into the learners' language system. Of less certainty is the role learner awareness plays in input enhancement, an issue that is of import given that Sharwood Smith's current term input enhancement (external manipulation) is derived from "language consciousness-raising" (an internal learning mechanism). Given this crucial role of attention and, to a lesser extent, awareness in the benefits of input enhancement, it is important to briefly review current approaches to the role of attention and awareness in SLA literature to better situate input enhancement within this attentional framework.

Attention and Awareness in SLA

Given that attention and awareness potentially play important roles in input enhancement, it is useful to discuss briefly several major and less developed theoretical approaches (e.g., Robinson, 1995, 2003; Schmidt, 1990, 1993, 2001; Tomlin & Villa, 1994) to the roles of attention and awareness in second/foreign language learning, mainly in the formal classroom setting.

Tomlin and Villa's Functional Model of Input Processing in SLA

Tomlin and Villa (1994) propose a functionally-based, fine-grained analysis of attention based on cognitive science research. Their model of input processing for SLA postulates that attention has three components with neurological correlates: (1) alertness (an overall readiness to deal with incoming stimuli), (2) orientation (the direction of attentional resources to a certain type of stimuli), and (3) detection (the cognitive registration of stimuli). According to Tomlin and Villa, it is detection alone that is necessary for further processing of input and subsequent learning to take place. The other two components can enhance the chances that detection will occur, but neither is necessary. Crucial to understanding Tomlin and Villa's claims is that, in their model, detection does *not* imply awareness. Awareness is defined as "a particular state of mind in which an individual has undergone a specific subjective experience of some cognitive content or external stimulus" (Tomlin & Villa, 1994, p. 193). Recently, the utility of Tomlin and Villa's model has been questioned (Schmidt, 2001; Simard & Wong, 2001) with respect to its generalizability to the SLA field and being too general to be of use.

Schmidt's Noticing Hypothesis

Schmidt's noticing hypothesis (Schmidt, 1990, 1993, 2001) contrasts sharply with Tomlin and Villa's (1994) view that awareness is not necessary for learning. According to Schmidt, attention controls access to awareness and is responsible for noticing, which he says is "the necessary and sufficient condition for the conversion of input into intake" (Schmidt, 1993, p. 209). He views attention as being isomorphic with awareness and rejects the idea of learning without awareness. Awareness, according to Allport (1988), is demonstrated through (a) some resulting behavioral or cognitive change, (b) a report of the experience, or (c) metalinguistic description of an underlying rule. Moreover, Schmidt posits that, in addition to awareness at the level of noticing, which leads to mere intake, there is another higher level of awareness, which he refers to as awareness at the level of understanding. Schmidt proposes that this level of awareness leads to deeper learning marked by restructuring and system learning since it is characterized by learners' ability to analyze, compare, and test hypotheses.

Robinson's Model of the Relationship between Attention and Memory

A third model of attention proposed in SLA is that of Robinson (1995). Robinson's model reconciles Tomlin and Villa's (1994) notion of detection (which does not involve awareness) and Schmidt's (1990 and elsewhere) notion of noticing, which involves awareness.

In Robinson's model, detection is posited to be an early stage in the process, sequentially prior to noticing. Noticing, in Robinson's model, is "detection plus rehearsal in short-term memory, prior to encoding in long-term memory" (Robinson, 1995, p. 296). Robinson, then, supports Schmidt's hypothesis that noticing does involve awareness and that it is crucial for learning to take place. At the same time, Robinson does not reject Tomlin and Villa's notion of detection but simply relegates it to an earlier stage in the learning process, thereby giving Schmidt's noticing hypothesis a more important role in input processing.

Awareness and Learning

As can be seen from the different theoretical models of attention, the facilitative role of attention in L2 development is generally accepted, but the role of awareness is not without debate. Specifically, Schmidt's noticing hypothesis and Robinson's model of the relationship between attention and memory posit a crucial role for awareness, whereas Tomlin and Villa's functional model of input processing does not. What is not controversial is that attentional resources may be allocated to a specific linguistic item in the input, but whether learner awareness is required for the grammatical information to be processed by the learner is open to debate. Several researchers have supported a dissociation between learning and awareness (e.g., Curran & Keele, 1993; Tomlin & Villa, 1994) while others have rejected this dissociation (Leow, 2000; Robinson, 1995; Schmidt, 1990 and elsewhere).

Empirical Studies of the Role of Awareness in L2 Development

A number of empirical SLA studies have provided support for the role of awareness and the differential effects of higher levels of awareness in SLA. Overall, these studies appear to provide empirical support for the facilitative effects of awareness on foreign language behavior and learning. More specifically, the main findings indicate that (a) awareness at the level of noticing and understanding contributed substantially to a significant increase in learners' ability to take in the targeted form or structure (Leow, 1997a, 2000, 2001a; Rosa & Leow, 2004a; Rosa & O'Neill, 1999) and produce in writing the targeted form or structure (Leow, 1997a, 2001a; Rosa & Leow, 2004a), including novel exemplars (Rosa & Leow, 2004a); (b) awareness at the level of understanding led to significantly more intake when compared to awareness at the level of noticing (Leow, 1997a, 2001a; Rosa & Leow, 2004a; Rosa &

O'Neill, 1999); (c) there is a correlation between awareness at the level of understanding and usage of hypothesis testing/rule formation (Leow, 1997a, 2000, 2001a; Rosa & Leow, 2004a; Rosa & O'Neill, 1999); (d) there is a correlation between level of awareness and formal instruction and directions to search for a rule (Rosa & O'Neill, 1999); and (e) there is a correlation between awareness at the level of understanding and learning conditions providing an explicit pretask (with grammatical explanation) as well as implicit or explicit concurrent feedback (Rosa & Leow, 2004a).

Theoretical Underpinnings of Input Enhancement

As mentioned above, input enhancement was derived from Sharwood Smith's original term "language consciousness-raising" (Sharwood Smith, 1981), a term that was initially framed in a discussion of Krashen's (1979) and Bialystok's (1978) views on the relationship between explicit knowledge (a conscious analytic awareness of the formal properties of the target language), and implicit knowledge (an intuitive feeling for what is correct and acceptable). Language consciousness-raising was, according to Sharwood Smith (1981), a teacher's guidance to promote learners' self discovery or conscious awareness of the formal features of the L2. In an effort to move away from the perception of consciousness-raising as "a complete and unrelenting focus on the formal structure of the TL" (Sharwood Smith, 1981, p. 160), Sharwood Smith proposed that language consciousness-raising be viewed from two axes: degrees of elaboration and explicitness.

It appears that the initial focus of the discussion on consciousness-raising was more on product (explicit knowledge) than on process (input processing). From an attentional perspective, the conscious analytic awareness of the formal properties of the target language appears to be relatively similar to Schmidt's (1990 and elsewhere) notion of awareness at the level of understanding that has been substantiated by empirical instances of hypothesis testing and rule formation found at the level of awareness in SLA research (e.g., Leow, 1997a; Rosa & Leow, 2004a; Rosa & O'Neill, 1999). Indeed, the data on awareness at the level of understanding gathered in studies employing concurrent data elicitation procedures (e.g., think aloud protocols) (e.g., Leow, 1997a, 2001a; Leow et al., 2003; Rosa & Leow, 2004a; Rosa & O'Neill, 1999) appear to equate more with the notion of "self discovery," in which learners arrive at the underlying rule of the targeted form or structure while interacting with L2 input, than with the provision of metalinguistic information by the teacher.

In 1991, Sharwood Smith appeared to view input enhancement somewhat more from an input processing perspective than a product perspective as previously posited. First of all, he overrode his previous term consciousness-raising with input enhancement while acknowledging the discrepancy in the two terms' assumptions regarding the input/intake dichotomy in light of an internal processing (consciousness-raising) versus an external manipulation of L2 input (input enhancement). In other words, while consciousness-raising assumed that learners became conscious of all the input they were exposed to, leading to some linguistic change in their mental state, input enhancement assumed that manipulated input (by the teacher) may or may not be taken in by the learners. Secondly, his postulation that input enhancement might also be learner-centered appears to suggest a more positive role for awareness, that is, learners do need to pay attention to and, additionally, become aware of the enhanced form or structure in the input before the form or structure is further processed into the learner language system. In his Figure 2, depicting the role of both external (teacher-centered) and internal (learner-centered) variables in whether enhanced input is indeed noticed by the learner, Sharwood Smith posited that what is taken in is "language input as registered by the learning mechanisms or, more generally, in learner's awareness" (Sharwood Smith, 1991, p. 121). From this description, it is quite arguable that consciousness or awareness (as currently employed in SLA literature) plays at least some theoretical role in the notion of input enhancement with respect to both L2 behavior (intake) and learner knowledge. Minimally, from an attentional perspective, it may be argued that awareness at the level of noticing (Schmidt, 1990 and elsewhere) may account for what is being postulated by Sharwood Smith in 1991.

Sharwood Smith cautioned that enhanced input might or might not be further processed into the language system, that is, L2 knowledge. In other words, while enhanced input is noticed and taken in by the learner, such linguistic information may not be further processed due to the kind of evidence to which learners are exposed.

However, in this same article, Sharwood Smith also began to question the role of awareness in input enhancement by drawing on notions from non-SLA fields such as "disunity of awareness" (Jackendoff, 1987), or the possibility of being aware of something and not aware of it, and suggested that language learning be viewed also from a modular perspective (Fodor, 1983). These issues are elaborated in his 1993 article in which he followed Jackendoff's (1987) postulation that no activity of the mind is conscious and that, at most, one is only aware of a succession of states. Further, any conscious introspection is taken care of by a separate language introspection processor. This perspective, according to Sharwood Smith, neatly fit in with the notion of modularity, or that language learner behavior is driven not by a single, complex system but by a battery of separate systems operating on different principles.

To this end, Sharwood Smith (1993) appeared to view the role of awareness in input processing as playing a reduced role in input enhancement. "In this way the role of awareness is vastly reduced from that which we might otherwise assume to be the case" (p. 171). From a current attentional perspective, one plausible interpretation of this statement may be that Sharwood Smith is backing away from a strong postulation of a role for awareness at the level of understanding (consciousness-raising) and is now proposing a reduced level of awareness, perhaps at the level of noticing, that is, attention plus a low level of awareness (cf., Schmidt's noticing hypothesis, 1990 and elsewhere above). Another interpretation may be that Sharwood Smith would agree with Tomlin and Villa's (1994) notion of detection, which is attention minus awareness. Current attentional research (e.g., Leow, 1997a, 2001a; Rosa & Leow, 2004a; Rosa & O'Neill, 1999) appears to provide empirical evidence for the role of awareness in SLA by reporting on both awareness at the level of noticing and higher levels of awareness (at the level of understanding) that lead to exemplars of hypothesis testing and rule formation, which is arguably similar to Sharwood Smith's original reference to learners' self discovery or conscious awareness of the formal features of the L2.

To conclude, while attention in input enhancement is generally accepted as playing a crucial role in L2 development, the role awareness plays remains unspecified but certainly not eliminated from theoretical consideration. The next sections discuss current research in relation to the roles of attention and awareness in input enhancement.

Input Enhancement Studies: The Role of Attention

Studies purporting to address the benefits of input enhancement over unenhanced input have generally followed Sharwood Smith's (1991) definition of input enhancement as any pedagogical intervention on the part of the teacher to make targeted items in the L2 input more salient in an effort to draw learners' attention to these enhanced items. In other words, studies in the research strand of input enhancement are minimally premised on the role of attention, that is, learners exposed to enhanced input should pay more attention to and substantially process better enhanced items in the input when compared to learners not exposed to such enhancement.

Several studies have attempted to address a permutation of the different exemplars of Sharwood Smith's two axes: elaboration and explicitness. According to Sharwood Smith, exemplars on the elaboration axis range from a onetime signal to indicate a learner error to repeated signals for the same type of error. Exemplars on the explicitness axis range from a facial gesture to a metalinguistically sophisticated rule explanation. However, the definition of input enhancement, based on the two axes (elaboration and explicitness) provided by Sharwood Smith, is arguably too open-ended to be empirically tested and this may have led to several misinterpretations of what comprises an empirical study with an appropriate research design to address the effects of input enhancement on comprehension, intake, and L2 development. Not surprisingly, then, what constitutes input enhancement has been interpreted from several perspectives that include (1) visually enhanced written input via the use of bolding, capitalizing, underlining, italicizing, different fonts and sizes, and so on (e.g., Alanen, 1995; Bowles, 2003; Izumi, 2002; Jourdenais, 1998; Jourdenais, Ota, Stauffer, Boyson, & Doughty, 1995; Leow, 1997b; Leow, Egi, Nuevo, & Tsai, 2003; Overstreet, 1998; Shook, 1994, 1999; White, 1998), (2) input enhancement (metalinguistic or visual) subsumed within some type of instruction, be it focus on form (e.g., Leeman, Arteagoitia, Fridman, & Doughty, 1995) or processing instruction (e.g., VanPatten & Cadierno, 1993), (3) input enhancement subsumed in oral interaction via the use of recasts (Leeman, 2003) or corrective feedback (e.g., White, Spada, Lightbown, & Ranta, 1991), (4) metalinguistic discussion of targeted grammatical structures in groups (e.g., Fotos, 1993), and (5) input enhancement as an overdose or increase of targeted forms or structures in the input by, for example, input flooding (e.g., Williams & Evans, 1998).

The mere fact that the notion of input enhancement permeates quite a large number of research strands in pedagogical SLA supports the notion that its definition is too broad to investigate exactly whether such external manipulation of the L2 input is beneficial to comprehension, intake, and L2 development. From a methodological viewpoint, two major internal validity limitations of most of the studies that have purported to have addressed the effects of input enhancement are (1) the failure to operationalize and measure the process of attention upon which the notion of input enhancement is unarguably based; in other words, the absence of concurrent data that established that attention was indeed paid to the enhanced forms in the input before any statistical analyses were conducted to address its effect (cf., Leow, 1999 for a critical overview of studies premised on the role of attention in L2 development) and (2) the conflation of input enhancement with one or more independent variables (especially in the instructional strands of research such as processing instruction and focus on form) that prevents any definitive statement to be made on the effect of the variable input enhancement.

Studies Employing Concurrent Data Elicitation Procedures

Current studies employing concurrent data elicitation procedures (think aloud protocols or verbal reports) may be useful not only to address the methodological need to operationalize and measure the process of attention (internal validity) but also to glean insights into how learners process enhanced input. Only four studies to date (Alanen, 1995; Bowles, 2003; Leow, 2001b; Leow et al., 2003) have employed think aloud protocols or verbal reports to establish learner attention to enhanced or unenhanced items. A fifth (Izumi, 2002) measured noticing via note-taking during exposure to L2 input, a measurement that may be subjected to critique due to the qualitatively poor data it might have provided. Attentional data were typically elicited via the use of nonmetalinguistic think aloud protocols, that is, learners were asked to think aloud without providing any metalinguistic explanation on their thoughts while interacting with the L2 input. With the exception of Alanen (1995), who conflated her concurrent data with offline data (sentence completion, grammatical judgment, and rule statements), the data elicited from the think aloud protocols of the other three studies revealed that reported noticing of targeted forms was statistically similar in the enhanced and unenhanced conditions, which may provide convincing evidence to support similar results in the majority of studies investigating the effects of input enhancement on L2 comprehension and L2 development. In addition, these concurrent data also revealed that learners did not necessarily attempt to process enhanced items for linguistic information but simply to extract semantic information from the targeted forms. This is not surprising given that the instructions typically requested that learners read or listen to the L2 input for information and, in a few cases, pay attention to the grammatical items (e.g., Shook, 1994). The richness of qualitative data gathered from think aloud protocols is clearly superior to data gathered after exposure (cf., Leow, 2000 for further elaboration of the merits of the use of both quantitative and qualitative analyses in SLA research).

Input Enhancement: The Role of Awareness

To date, there is no study that has empirically addressed whether awareness plays a role in input enhancement in promoting superior comprehension, intake, and L2 development. Clearly, to conduct such research, the use of concurrent data elicitation procedures such as think aloud protocols[1] will be required. At the same time, it is instructive to review what studies that have employed such elicitation procedures have revealed in regard to the issue of awareness.

Leow (2001a) was the first empirical SLA study on textual input enhancement to employ both concurrent (during exposure) and offline data collection procedures to establish that participants noticed targeted forms in the input. These data were used in conjunction with scores from immediate and delayed recognition and production tasks to determine whether textual input enhancement had significant benefits over unenhanced input. Leow reported that no significant benefit was found for input enhancement either for (1) amount of reported noticing (the noticing hypothesis), (2) comprehension, or (3) intake.

While the results of this study may lay claim to the role of awareness in input enhancement, of even more interest regarding this issue were the findings reported regarding the performances of the two high performers in both enhanced and unenhanced conditions. Both of these participants were coded as demonstrating a level of meta-awareness (cf., Leow, 1997a, 2001a for a definition of different levels of awareness in SLA) that included conceptually-driven processing usually associated with the more sophisticated cognitive processes of hypothesis testing, metalinguistic description of the targeted forms, and rule formation (awareness at the level of understanding) (cf., Leow 1997a; Rosa & Leow, 2004a; Rosa & O'Neill, 1999). As discussed above, these features may be arguably reflective of Sharwood Smith's original notion of consciousness-raising that denotes learners' self discovery or conscious awareness of the formal features of the L2 and may be explicated within an attentional framework.

Interestingly, Leow (2001a) concluded that the role of level of awareness and not necessarily input enhancement might have been responsible for the differential results found between these two participants and the others in the study. According to Leow, "noticing in discourse, then, may not necessarily contribute to a more profound processing of grammatical information, that is, beyond intake, unless accompanied minimally by a level of meta-awareness" (p. 505). This statement is further supported by the findings that 55% and over of the participants in both enhanced and unenhanced conditions scored zero on the written production task while 85% and over scored two or less out of a total of 17 items. Taken together, the perceived belief that enhanced input may draw learners' attention to more salient forms in the input with the potential of being further processed beyond intake into the learners' language system may need to be reexamined. A methodological issue here is whether production tasks are indeed adequate to address whether learners minimally noticed and processed enhanced input at the level of intake.

Bowles (2003) replicated Leow (2001a) at the intermediate level and, while she found similar results (no significant effect of enhancement), she also reported that online data further revealed that more participants in the enhanced group made meta-linguistic comments about targeted forms than did participants in the unenhanced group (71% in the enhanced group vs. 38% in the unenhanced group). She concluded that enhanced input promoted meta-linguistic comment more than unenhanced input did.

Conclusion

Given the central role of attention in the current definition of input enhancement and the potential role awareness plays based on the original definition, this chapter has attempted to situate input enhancement within an attentional framework from both an attention and an awareness perspective, and to discuss some of the methodological issues associated with this strand of research in pedagogical SLA literature.

It has shown that while attention remains central to the notion of input enhancement, the role awareness plays appears to be reduced but not completely eliminated from the definition.

It has been argued that the term "input enhancement" is too broad to investigate empirically its so-called effects on L2 comprehension, intake, and L2 development and care should be taken in assuming that once a study has included some exemplar of input enhancement, this study has empirically investigated its (non) effectiveness. The chapter has also provided a brief overview of studies that have been cited in the literature as input enhancement studies. It has been pointed out that most of the research on the so-called notion of input enhancement suffers from internal validity limitations, namely, a failure to establish empirically that learner attention to the enhanced items was indeed paid before its effects could be statistically measured. At the same time, studies employing concurrent data elicitation procedures such as think alouds have reported that (1) the nonsignificant difference in performance found in many studies may be due to a similar amount of reported noticing of the enhanced forms in the input and (2) learners exposed to enhanced input may be processing such data with a low level of awareness, which may not necessarily contribute to a more profound processing of grammatical information, that is, beyond intake, unless accompanied minimally by a higher level of awareness found to correlate positively with superior performance.

Finally, it is strongly recommended that future studies purporting to investigate the notion of input enhancement strive to tease out this variable in their research designs before making any claims on the benefits of input enhancement. Studies also need to be cautious in extrapolating the effects of input enhancement due to the multiplicity of variables that are involved in providing definitive statements regarding its effects (e.g., level of language experience, type of linguistic item, amount of exposure, etc.). The roles of attention and awareness in input enhancement clearly warrant future research in order to contribute to our understanding of its effects and also explicate the theoretical foundation(s) of input enhancement in L2 comprehension, intake, and L2 development.

Questions and Topics for Discussion

1) The issue of awareness is quite a controversial topic in current SLA literature. Based on the findings of current empirical studies

reported above, what role do you think awareness plays in input enhancement?
2) We all, as teachers, enhance L2 input, be it underlining a word on the blackboard, stressing a specific word etc., in the classroom. What are our learning expectations for employing such enhancement? Now, based on the information above, what do you think L2 learners do when exposed to enhanced input?
3) The majority of studies isolating the variable input enhancement appear to provide no significant, statistical superiority of input enhancement over unenhanced input. What are some additional factors that may play a role in explicating these findings?
4) Given question 3, should teachers cease from providing enhanced input to their students? What are the advantages and disadvantages, if any?

Notes

1) See Leow and Morgan-Short (2004) and Bowles and Leow (2005) for empirical support for the use of think-aloud protocols as one kind of concurrent data elicitation procedure. In these studies, comparing a think-aloud and a nonthink-aloud group revealed no significant effect for the issue of reactivity, that is, the potential detrimental impact of thinking aloud while performing a task.
2) Of course, given the relatively broad scope of what apparently constitutes input enhancement, an argument may be made that any task designed to draw learners' attention to targeted features in the input (e.g., the problem-solving tasks found in Leow, 1997a, 1998a, b, 2000, 2001a; Rosa & Leow, 2004a, b; Rosa & O'Neill, 1999) all fall under the rubric of input enhancement. However, these cited studies have been framed within an attentional framework and not within an input enhancement strand of research.

References

Alanen, R. (1995). Input enhancement and rule presentation in second language acquisition. In R.W. Schmidt (Ed.), *Attention and awareness in foreign language learning* (pp. 183-216). Honolulu: University of Hawai'i Press.

Allport, A. (1988). What concept of consciousness? In J. Marcel & E. Bisiach (Eds.), *Consciousness in contemporary science* (pp. 159-182). London: Claredon Press.

Bialystok, E. (1978). A theoretical model of second language learning. *Language Learning, 28*, 69-83.

Bowles, M. (2003). The effects of textual enhancement on language learning: An on-line/offline study of fourth-semester students. In P. Kempchinsky & C.E. Piñeros (Eds.), *Theory, practice, and acquisition: Papers from the 6th Hispanic Linguistics Symposium and the 5th Conference on the Acquisition of Spanish & Portuguese* (pp. 395-411). Summerville, MA: Cascadilla Press.

Bowles, M.A., & Leow, R.P. (2005). Reactivity and type of verbal report in SLA research methodology: Expanding the scope of investigation. *Studies in Second Language Acquisition, 27*, 415-440.

Curran, T. & Keele, S.W. (1993). Attentional and nonattentional forms of sequence learning. *Journal of Experimental Psychology: Learning, Memory, and Cognition, 19*, 189-202.

Fodor, J. (1983). *The modularity of mind*. Cambridge, MA: MIT Press.

Fotos, S. (1993). Consciousness-raising and noticing through focus on form: Grammar task development versus formal instruction. *Applied Linguistics, 14*, 385-407.

Izumi, S. (2002). Output, input enhancement, and the noticing hypothesis: An experimental study on ESL relativization. *Studies in Second Language Acquisition, 24*, 541-577.

Jackendoff, R. (1987). *Consciousness and the computational mind*. New York: Academic Press.

Jourdenais, R. (1998). *The effects of textual enhancement on the acquisition of the Spanish preterit and imperfect*. Unpublished doctoral dissertation, Georgetown University.

Jourdenais, R., Ota, M., Stauffer, S., Boyson, B., & Doughty, C. (1995). Does textual enhancement promote noticing?: A think aloud protocol analysis. In R.W. Schmidt (Ed.), *Attention and awareness in foreign language learning* (pp. 183-216). Honolulu: University of Hawai'i, Second Language Teaching and Curriculum Center.

Krashen, S. (1979). A response to McLaughlin 'The monitor model, some methodological considerations.' *Language Learning, 29*, 151-167.

Leeman, J. (2003). Recasts and second language development: Beyond negative feedback. *Studies in Second Language Acquisition, 22*, 37-63.

Leeman, J., Arteagoitia, I., Fridman, B., & Doughty, C. (1995). Integrating attention to form with meaning: Focus on form in content-based Spanish instruction. In R.W. Schmidt (Ed.), *Attention and awareness in foreign language learning* (pp. 217-258). Honolulu: University of Hawai'i, Second Language Teaching and Curriculum Center.

Leow, R. (1997a). The effects of input enhancement and text length on adult L2 readers' comprehension and intake in second language acquisition. *Applied Language Learning, 8*, 151-182.

Leow, R. (1997b). Attention, awareness, and foreign language behavior. *Language Learning, 47*, 467-506.

Leow, R. (1998a). Toward operationalizing the process of attention in SLA: Evidence for Tomlin and Villa's (1994) fine-grained analysis of attention. *Applied Psycholinguistics, 19*, 133-159.

Leow, R. (1998b). The effects of amount and type of exposure on adult learners' L2 development. *Modern Language Journal, 82*, 49-68.

Leow, R. (1999). The role of attention in second/foreign language classroom research: Methodological issues. In F. Martínez-Gil, & J. Gutiérrez-Rexach (Eds.), *Advances in Hispanic Linguistics: Papers from the 2nd Hispanic Linguistics Symposium* (pp. 60-71). Somerville, MA: Cascadilla Press.

Leow, R. (2000). A study of the role of awareness in foreign language behavior: Aware vs. unaware learners. *Studies in Second Language Acquisition, 22*, 557-584.

Leow, R. (2001a). Do learners notice enhanced forms while interacting with the L2 input? An online and offline study of the role of written input enhancement in L2 reading. *Hispania, 84*, 496-509.

Leow, R.P. (2001b). Attention, awareness and foreign language behavior. *Language Learning, 51*, 113-155.

Leow, R.P., Egi, T., Nuevo, A-M., & Tsai, Y. (2003). The roles of textual enhancement and type of linguistic item in adult L2 learners' comprehension and intake. *Applied Language Learning, 13*, 93-108.

Leow, R.P., & Morgan-Short, K. (2004). To think aloud or not to think aloud: The issue of reactivity in SLA research methodology. *Studies in Second Language Acquisition, 26*, 35-57.

Overstreet, M.H. (1998). Text enhancement and content familiarity: The focus of learner attention. *Spanish Applied Linguistics, 2*, 229-258.

Robinson, P. (1995). Review article: Attention, memory, and the noticing hypothesis. *Language Learning, 45*, 283-331.

Robinson, P. (2003). Attention and memory during SLA. In C. Doughty, & M. Long (Eds.), *Handbook of research in second language acquisition*. Oxford: Blackwell.

Rosa, E., & Leow, R. (2004a). Awareness, different learning conditions, and L2 development. *Applied Psycholinguistics, 25*, 269-292.

Rosa, E., & Leow, R. (2004b). Computerized task-based exposure, explicitness and type of feedback on Spanish L2 development. *Modern Language Journal, 88*, 192-217.

Rosa, E., & O'Neill, M. (1999). Explicitness, intake, and the issue of awareness: Another piece to the puzzle. *Studies in Second Language Acquisition, 21*, 511-556.

Schmidt, R.W. (1990). The role of consciousness in second language learning. *Applied Linguistics, 11*, 129-158.

Schmidt, R.W. (1993). Awareness and second language acquisition. *Annual Review of Applied Linguistics, 13*, 206-226.

Schmidt, R. (2001). Attention. In P. Robinson (Ed.), *Cognition and second language instruction* (pp. 3-32). New York: Cambridge University Press.

Sharwood Smith, M. (1981). Consciousness-raising and the second language learner. *Applied Linguistics, 2*, 159-168.

Sharwood Smith, M. (1991). Speaking to many minds: On the relevance of different types of language information for the L2 learner. *Second Language Research, 17*, 118-136.

Sharwood Smith, M. (1993). Input enhancement in instructed SLA: Theoretical bases. *Studies in Second Language Acquisition, 15*, 165-179.

Shook, D.J. (1994). FL/L2 reading, grammatical information, and the input-to-intake phenomenon. *Applied Language Learning, 5*, 57-93.

Shook, D.J. (1999). What foreign language reading recalls reveal about the input-to-intake phenomenon. *Applied Language Learning, 10*, 39-76.

Simard, D., & Wong, W. (2001). Alertness, orientation, and detection. *Studies in Second Language Acquisition, 23*, 103-124.

Tomlin, R.S., & Villa, V. (1994). Attention in cognitive science and second language acquisition. *Studies in Second Language Acquisition, 16*, 183-203.

VanPatten, B., & Cadierno, T. (1993). Input processing and second language acquisition: A role for instruction. *Modern Language Journal, 77*, 45-57.

White, J. (1998). Getting the learners' attention: A typographical input enhancement study. In C. Doughty, & J. Williams (Eds.), *Focus on form in classroom second language acquisition* (pp. 85-113). Cambridge: Cambridge University Press.

White, L., Spada, N., Lightbown, P., & Ranta, L. (1991). Input enhancement and L2 question formation. *Applied Linguistics, 4*, 416-432.

Williams, J., & Evans, J. (1998). What kind of focus and on which forms? In C. Doughty & J. Williams (Eds.), *Focus on form in classroom second language acquisition* (pp. 139-155). Cambridge: Cambridge University Press.

Chapter 4
Focus on Form Through Recasts in Dyadic Student-Teacher Interaction: A Case for Recast Enhancement

Hossein Nassaji, University of Victoria

The assumption that L2 learners need to attend to both form and meaning in order to acquire an L2 has become fundamental to current theory and research in second language acquisition. One way of providing learners with such form-meaning opportunities is through interactional feedback, that is, feedback provided by means of various negotiation strategies such as clarification requests, confirmation checks, repetitions, and recasts during conversational interaction (Long, 1996). These strategies have been suggested as a means of providing learners with negotiation of meaning opportunities and information about the potential ungrammaticality of utterances (e.g., Gass, Mackey, & Pica, 1998; Long, 1996; Long, Inagaki, & Ortega, 1998; Long & Robinson, 1998; Mackey & Oliver, 2002; Mackey, Oliver, & Leeman, 2003; Mackey & Philp, 1998; Pica, 1994, 1996).

A number of SLA researchers have recently examined the role of interactional feedback and its various types in second language development (e.g., Doughty & Varela, 1998; Iwashita, 2001, 2003; Mackey & Oliver, 2002; Mackey et al., 2003; Mackey & Philp, 1998; McDonough

& Mackey, 2000; Oliver & Mackey, 2003). Among all feedback types examined, recasts have received the most attention. **Recasts** are defined as utterances that correctly reformulate an interlocutor's erroneous utterance by changing the erroneous part, while maintaining the intended meaning (e.g., Braidi, 1995, 2002; Long, 1996; Lyster & Ranta, 1997; Mackey & Philp, 1998). However, studies that have investigated the occurrence and usefulness of recasts in both classroom and non-classroom settings have produced mixed results. While some have found evidence that recasts can provide the type of negative feedback and focus on form necessary for L2 development (e.g., Carroll & Swain, 1993; Doughty & Varela, 1998; Leeman, 2003; Mackey & Philp, 1998), others have shown that although recasts are widely used in language classrooms, they are not very effective in comparison to other types of more explicit interactive feedback (e.g., Lyster, 1998; Lyster & Ranta, 1997).

A number of studies have investigated the effectiveness of recasts in observational classroom research. A study conducted by Lyster and Ranta (1997), for example, focused on French immersion learners. Analyzing 18.3 hours of classroom interaction, the researchers found that while recasts accounted for more than half of the feedback types (55%), it was the least effective type, leading to only 18% repair following feedback. Other types of feedback such as elicitation, clarification requests, metalinguistic feedback, and explicit correction, though less frequent, were found to be more effective, leading to 46%, 27%, 45%, 36%, and 31% repair, respectively. In a similar study, Panova and Lyster (2002) examined the role of corrective feedback in an adult ESL classroom. They also found that while recasts were frequently used, the rate of learner repair following recasts remained low. In another study Ellis, Basturkmen, and Loewen (2001) examined the occurrence of interactional feedback in an adult ESL context in New Zealand. These researchers found not only frequent use of recasts in these ESL contexts, but also a much higher rate of uptake (71.6%) for recasts than the rate found by Lyster and Ranta (1997).

In addition to observation research, several studies have investigated the role of recasts in experimental contexts (e.g., Carroll & Swain, 1993; Doughty & Varela, 1998; Gass et al., 1998; Han, 2002; Long et al., 1998; Mackey & Philp, 1998). Doughty and Valera (1998), for example, examined the role of recasts in two middle school content-based science classes. One class was used as an experimental group, receiving corrective feedback in the form of recasts, and the other as a control group, receiving no corrective feedback. The target structure was the English past tense. The researchers found that recasts were highly effective in facilitating the learning of the target structure, particularly when they were preceded by an utterance that repeated the error with rising intonation or stress. Mackey and Philp (1998) conducted an experimental study in which they compared the performance of groups of L2 learners who received interactionally modified input with those who received intensive recasts. Focusing on the development of question formation as a measure of L2 development, they found that advanced learners benefited more from interaction that contained intensive recasts than interaction that did not. They concluded that despite the evidence for the ineffectiveness of recasts, recasts could be beneficial for short-term learning.

Another experimental study on the role of recasts was conducted by Long, Inagaki, and Ortega (1998). These researchers designed two experiments to investigate the role of recasts versus models among Japanese and Spanish learners of English. The target forms in Spanish were object topicalization and adverb placement; those in Japanese were the ordering of adjectives and locative constructions. The results of this study were mixed. The Japanese learners who received recasts did not show improvement on either target forms. The Spanish learners who received recasts pertaining to adverb placement outperformed those who received models. However, this effect was not found for object topicalization.

As can be seen, studies that have investigated the role of recasts have reported different results, with observational studies in content-based classrooms reporting a less positive effect for recasts than experimental studies. Some researchers have attributed the low rate of success in meaning-based classroom settings to the ambiguity of recasts and learners' difficulty in perceiving recasts as corrective feedback (e.g., Chaudron, 1977; Lyster, this volume; Lyster & Ranta, 1997; Pica, 2002). Lyster and Ranta (1997), for example, suggested that in content-based classrooms, because the primary focus is on meaning, students may not notice the difference between their erroneous utterance and the teacher's utterance in the feedback. Students may not know whether the teacher is using the recast to seek confirmation of the content or to provide corrective feedback. On the other hand, in experimental research, because of its controlled nature, the focus of the recast may become more prominent and more salient for the learner than in non-experimental research; thus, learners' attention may be directed more effectively to the target form in the feedback. Indeed, in a reanalysis of the database used in Lyster and Ranta (1997), Lyster (1998) found that in content-based classrooms, teachers not only recasted erroneous forms but also repeated or rephrased non-erroneous forms, and the rephrasing and repeating of non-erroneous utterances was highly similar in type and distribution to the recasting of erroneous utterances. These similarities led him to conclude that "the formal properties entailed in the corrective reformulations may easily be overridden by their functional properties in meaning oriented classrooms." (p. 65).

The question that arises here is whether there are ways to disambiguate the functions of recasts so that they can be better noticed as corrective feedback and can more effectively direct learners' attention to the form in focus. Based on the assumption that increasing the salience of input may facilitate its selection and processing in language acquisition (e.g., Sharwood Smith, 1993), the present study analyzed data from task-based student-teacher interaction to identify the different types of recasts used, and explore whether the enhancement of recasts through additional prompts (e.g., rising intonation, word stress, or question words and phrases that invite the learner to respond) increases their salience and makes learners more likely to modify their non-target output in response to feedback.

Methods

The data for this study come from a larger research project on the role of interactive feedback in task-based teacher-student interaction. Participants were 42 adult ESL students and two English language teachers. The learners came from different L1 language backgrounds including Cantonese, Chinese, French, Japanese, Korean, Portuguese, Spanish, and Thai. There were 26 males and 16 females and their ages ranged from 18 to 35 (M=23.42). All had recently arrived in Canada and were studying English in an intensive ESL program in a university context. Their amount of prior English study ranged from 3 to 18 months. Based on the results of their classroom placement tests, the participants were considered intermediate ESL learners. Both teachers had TESL certificates, ESL teaching experience, and were pursuing undergraduate degrees in applied linguistics.

Data Collection Procedure

Each learner participated in task-based dyadic interaction with one of the teachers and received various forms of explicit and implicit interactive feedback on their erroneous and non-erroneous utterances. Each learner met individually with a teacher in a small room equipped with a microphone and a digital audio-recorder connected to a computer terminal and completed a communicative task. The task was a picture sequencing task in which the learner received, in random order, four pictures, each depicting a particular scene. The learner had to arrange the pictures into a sequence that he or she believed represented the event and then describe it orally to the teacher. The teacher received the same pictures plus two additional ones similar to the others in terms of scene characteristics. The teacher had to communicate with the learner in order to reconstruct the event based on the student's description. Prior to the study, the two teachers were trained in providing different types of interactional feedback, including recasts.

Transcription and Coding

The audio-recorded data were transcribed after the interaction using normal orthography. For inclusiveness and clarity, the written transcriptions were then reviewed and checked against the audio recordings by a second transcriber. To ensure reliability and consistency of coding, the transcribed data were first coded by a trained research assistant. Next, a random sample of 10% of the data were coded by the author. The lower inter-rater reliability obtained at all levels of analysis was 91%.

The data coding was conducted in three stages. First the entire database was segmented into interactional feedback exchanges. To delineate the exchanges, a three-move model of conversational discourse was used according to which a conversational exchange includes three possible moves: an initiation move, a feedback move, and a response move (Chaudron, 1977; Nassaji & Wells, 2000; Oliver, 2000). Once the interactional exchanges were identified, the constituent moves within each feedback exchange were examined and coded.

The initial analysis involved the examination of student utterances preceding feedback and their categorization into erroneous and non-erroneous utterances. Student utterances were coded as erroneous if they included at least one non-target-like form. If it did not contain any errors, the utterance was coded as non-erroneous. The teachers' utterances following students' erroneous utterances were examined and coded for type of feedback. Following Braidi (2002), the teachers' feedback was first classified into two broad categories: recasts and non-recasts. **Recasts** were defined as any utterance that included a target-like reformulation of a learner's erroneous form including those that both provided and sought confirmation of the message. **Non-recasts** were feedback moves that contained other kinds of feedback including clarification requests, metalinguistic cues, explicit corrections, and content negotiation moves.

Because the focus of the study was on recasts, after cataloguing the general types of recasts, each one was closely examined to identify the different ways in which it had been provided. This examination showed that in some cases the teachers recasted a learner's erroneous utterance in the form of a simple declarative statement, used mainly to confirm message comprehensibility (see Lyster, 1998). In other cases, the teachers combined recasts with other intonational prompts such as rising intonation or added stress, and yet in still other cases, they used explicit verbal prompts such as "do you mean," or "is that what you mean," etc. In the latter case, the recasts took the form of **pushed output**, that is, utterances that push the learner towards producing a more accurate or comprehensible form of output. These additional intonational and word-related prompts were assumed to increase the perceptual salience of the recast and the possibility of it being noticed by the learner (Leeman, 2003). Therefore, I called them **recast enhancement prompts**. Then, depending on the presence or absence of the prompts and their types, I categorized the recasts into the following three categories: unenhanced recasts, intonationally enhanced recasts, and verbally enhanced recasts.

Unenhanced recasts reformulated the learners' erroneous utterances but were declarative and included no intonational or verbal prompts. This type of recast was mainly used to either acknowledge receipt of the message or to confirm message comprehensibility with no additional prompts.

Example 1 (S=student, T=teacher)
S: And they found out the one woman run away.
T: OK, the woman was running away.
S: Running away.

Intonationally enhanced recasts reformulated the learners' erroneous utterances, but were also enhanced with additional intonational prompts such as word stress and rising intonation.

> Example 2 (S=student, T=teacher)
> S: And she catched her.
> T: She CAUGHT [stressed] her?
> S: Yeah, caught her.

Verbally enhanced recasts reformulated the learners' erroneous utterances, but were also enhanced with explicit verbal prompts such as "do you mean," "is that what you mean," etc.

> Example 3 (S=student, T=teacher)
> S: She wear glasses and uh.
> T: Do you mean she is wearing glasses?
> S: Yeah, she's wearing glasses.

After coding the feedback moves, the learners' responses were coded as well. Responses were initially coded as repair or no repair. **Repair** was defined as a response that resulted in the successful modification of a learner's original utterance. Responses that did not result in successful modification of the original utterance were coded as **no repair**.

It is important to note that not all repair (or no repair) responses are the same. For example, while some repairs can be mere repetitions of the feedback, others can involve modification and incorporation of feedback. Similarly, while some no repairs can result from ignoring the teacher's feedback and simply continuing with the discourse topic, others can result from erroneous modification of an original error. Therefore, after coding the responses as repair or no repair, I further coded them for the nature of repair. For that purpose, I distinguished between two types of repair: **repair as repetition of feedback** and **repair as incorporation of feedback**, and four types of no repair: **repetition of output, partial modification of output, confirm/reject/acknowledge,** and **move on**. These categories are presented in Table 4.1 with definitions and examples from the database.

Results

Altogether a total of 339 learners' initiation utterances preceding feedback were coded, out of which 310 (91%) were erroneous and 29 (9%) were non-erroneous. Of the 310 erroneous utterances 141 (45%) were followed by recasts, and the remaining 169 (55%) were followed by non-recasts. Thus, recasts accounted for about half of the feedback moves in response to the learners' non-target-like utterances.

Of the total number of recasts (n=141), 39 (28%) were unenhanced recasts (i.e., recasts – prompts), 94 (66%) were intonationally enhanced recasts (i.e., recasts + intonational prompts), and 8 (6%) were verbally enhanced recasts (i.e., recasts + verbal prompts). This suggests that

Table 4.1. Framework for Coding the Nature of Repair

	Type of response	Definition	Example
Repair	Repetition of feedback	The response exactly repeats the feedback.	S: Skipping, running, the thief. T: She was running away. S: Yeah, running away.
	Incorporation of feedback	The response repairs the error not by repeating it, but rather by modifying and incorporating it into a longer utterance.*	S: There was a boy witness see the whole thing. T: A boy that saw the whole thing? S: Yeah, the boy saw the whole thing and he pointed to the girl before it was too late.
No repair	Repetition of output	The response repeats the original erroneous output.	S: And she hitted . . . T: She HIT? S: Yeah, hitted hitted the pickpockers.
	Partial modification of output	The response partially modifies the erroneous output thus leaving the utterance still in need of repair.	S: And they . . . the . . . three people pointed her. T: Three people are pointing at her. S: Pointing her.
	Confirm/reject/ acknowledge	The response confirms, rejects, or simply acknowledges the content of the feedback.	S: Her hair is bind above her head. T: Oh her hair is tied back. S: Yeah.
	Move on	The response continues the topic.	S: When they went through in front of bookstore. T: In front of the bookstore. S: A chief, chief suddenly ran away from them.

* = See Lyster and Ranta (1997) for similar categories of repair.

most of the time when the teachers recasted the learners' erroneous utterances, they used some kind of prompt, either intonational or verbal. A one way Chi-square analysis revealed that the difference between the frequencies of the three types of recasts was statistically significant: $Ç^2 (2, N = 141) = 80.72. p < .0001$.

One of the main questions in this study concerned the extent to which recasts were effective in leading to learners' immediate repair, and in particular, whether there were any differences between the effectiveness of different types of recasts in that regard. To address this question the frequencies of the learners' repairs in response to recasts in general, as well as in response to different types of recasts, were calculated. As Table 4.2 shows, out of all the recasts (n=141), only 48 (34%) led to successful repair and 93 (66%) led to no repair. Thus, in more than half of the cases, recasts were not effective in pushing learners to modify their erroneous output. An examination of the repair following each recast type, however, revealed differences. Specifically, it showed that of the three types of recasts, unenhanced recasts (i.e., recasts-prompts) led to the lowest rate of successful repair (10%). However, when recasts were enhanced with intonational prompts, the rate of successful repair increased to 41%, and when they were enhanced with verbal prompts the rate increased to 62%. A two way Chi-square analysis revealed a significant relationship between type of recast and type of response (repair vs. no repair): $Ç^2(2, N = 141) = 15.03, p < .001$.

The subsequent analyses examining the nature of *repair* and *no repair* responses are presented in Table 4.3. As the table shows, about half of the no repairs in the case of unenhanced recasts were move on responses (51%), suggesting that in many cases, this type of recast

Table 4.2. Frequency and Percentage of Learner Repair in Different Types of Recasts

Recasts	No repair	Repair	Total
Unenhanced	35	4	39
	90%	10%	28%
Intonationally enhanced	55	39	94
	59%	41%	66%
Verbally enhanced	3	5	8
	38%	62%	6%
Total	93	48	141
	66%	34%	100%

did not lead to any form of uptake. This could be because either the learners did not notice the feedback or, if they did, they did not believe it necessary to respond to it. As for the few repair responses, most involved repetition of the recasts (3 out of 4). In the case of intonationally enhanced recasts, only 27% of no repair responses were move on responses, suggesting that in most cases, this type of recast led to some kind of uptake. But more than half of the uptake involved yes-no (confirming/rejecting) responses or responses that simply acknowledged the content of the feedback (55%). This recast type, however, led to a higher rate of repair than the unenhanced recasts did, although the

Table 4.3. Type of Repair and Relationship with Recast

Types of Recasts		con/ rej/ack	incor of feed	move on	partial mod of output	rep of output	rep of feed	Total
Unenhanced	No repair	11 31%	0 0%	18 51%	6 17%	0 0%	0 0%	35 90%
	Repair	0 0%	1 25%	0 0%	0 0%	0 0%	3 75%	4 10%
	Total	11 28%	2 5%	18 46%	6 15%	0 0%	2 5%	39 100%
Intonationally enhanced	No repair	30 55%	0 0%	15 27%	4 7%	6 11%	0 0%	55 59%
	Repair	0 0%	10 26%	0 0%	0 0%	0 0%	29 74%	39 41%
	Total	30 32%	10 11%	15 16%	4 4%	6 6%	29 31%	94 100%
Verbally enhanced	No repair	0 0%	0 0%	0 0%	2 67%	1 33%	0 0%	3 38%
	Repair	0 0%	2 40%	0 0%	0 0%	0 0%	3 60%	5 63%
	Total	0 0%	3 38%	0 0%	2 25%	1 13%	2 25%	8 100%

Note: con/rej/ack = confirm/reject/acknowledge; partial mod of output = partial modification of output; incor of feed = incorporation of feedback; rep of feed = repetition of feedback; rep of output = repetition of error; move on = move on (topic continuation).

majority of repair responses involved repetitions of recasts (74%). As for the verbally enhanced recasts, there were no move on responses, suggesting that all instances of this recast type resulted in some form of uptake. Also 2 of the 3 no repair responses involved partial modification of the error. Of the 5 repair responses, most (3) involved repetition of feedback. Overall, the verbally enhanced recasts seem to be more effective in producing successful uptake and modified output. But we should note that the frequency of this type of recast was very low; hence, we do not know whether we would have the same percentage of modified output if we had more instances of this type of recast.

Note: con/rej/ack = confirm/reject/acknowledge; partial mod of output = partial modification of output; incor of feed = incorporation of feedback; rep of feed = repetition of feedback; rep of output = repetition of error; move on = move on (topic continuation).

Discussion and Conclusion

Although there has been controversy over the exact nature of attentional processes in SLA (Bialystok, 1990, 1994; Leow, 1997, 2002; Tomlin & Villa, 1994), many second language acquisition researchers now believe that attention to language forms plays an important role in language learning (e.g., Carroll & Swain, 1993; Doughty, 2001; Doughty & Varela, 1998; Ellis, 2001; Fotos, 1994; Fotos & Ellis, 1991; Nassaji, 1999; Nassaji & Fotos, 2004; Robinson, 1995; Schmidt, 1993, 1995, 2001; VanPatten, 2002). However, when it comes to recasts, due to their implicit nature, learners have been found to have difficulty noticing target forms (e.g., Lyster, 1998; Mackey, Gass, & McDonough, 2000; Morris & Tarone, 2003; Pica, 2002). Therefore, it is important to find ways to increase the salience of recasts so that they can be better noticed in general, and so that learners' attention can be better directed to forms in the feedback.

The findings of this study suggest that one way of doing so could be by combining recasts with additional intonational and verbal prompts. In this study, the analyses that examined the effectiveness of recasts in general indicated that in more than half of the cases, recasts were not effective in leading to successful repair. However, the analyses that compared the accuracy of learners' immediate repair in response to different types of recasts showed higher rates of accuracy in response to enhanced recasts (i.e., recasts used in conjunction with intonational and verbal prompts) than to unenhanced recasts (i.e., recasts that were used with no such prompts).

These findings underscore the importance of enhancing the focus of conversational recasts in second language student-teacher interaction and suggest that recasts must be salient enough to become useful for L2 learners. They also support the findings of a few previous studies that have provided evidence that when the salience of feedback becomes enhanced, particularly through the use of word stress or intonation, its effectiveness increases (Doughty & Varela, 1998; Leeman, 2003; McDonough, 2005). Leeman (2003), for example, found that recasts with enhanced salience contributed significantly to the learning of noun-adjective agreement among Spanish L2 learners. Doughty and Valera (1998) found that when recasts were used in conjunction with intonational prompts that pushed the learner to respond to feedback, recasts were highly effective in facilitating the learning of the English past tense. McDonough (2005) found that when clarification requests were combined with enhanced stress and repetition in response to learners' non-target-like questions, they lead to increased production of modified output following feedback.

The advantage of enhanced recasts may be attributed to learners' increased attention to the target form. It is possible that when recasts are combined with additional intonational or verbal prompts, learners may become better aware of the fact that there could be something wrong with their original utterance. These prompts may give the feedback more attentional focus; hence, making the learner more likely to attend and respond to feedback. On the other hand, when recasts involve no enhanced prompts or signals, the learner may take the feedback as a simple reaction to the message and thus may either not feel the need to respond or, if they do respond, their attention may be directed to the content of the message, rather than the non-targetness of their prior utterance.

A few caveats are in order. First, in this study, the effectiveness of recasts was measured in terms of learners' immediate repair following recasts. Although learners' immediate repair in response to feedback has been suggested to contribute to language learning (Chaudron, 1977; Ellis et al., 2001), as noted by several researchers, such immediate responses should not be taken as evidence that any language acquisition has taken place (Ellis et al., 2001; Gass & Varonis, 1994; Lyster & Ranta, 1997; Mackey & Philp, 1998). Language acquisition is a long-term phenomenon, and as Ellis et al. (2001) pointed out, in order to determine that it has taken place, it is necessary to show that the learner is able to produce the target forms spontaneously on subsequent occasions without any pushing or prompting.

Second, despite evidence for successful repair following recasts, in most cases the repair was mainly a mere repetition, rather than assimilation or incorporation, of feedback. In such cases, it is very difficult to judge whether or not the learner has made any real restructuring in his or her interlanguage knowledge.

Finally, in this study declarative unenhanced recasts occurred less frequently than recasts that were intonationlly enhanced. However, in his study of content-based French immersion classrooms, Lyster (1998) found that declarative recasts accounted for the majority of recast types. Lyster also found that declarative recasts invited more repair than interrogative recasts. In this study, however, declarative (unenhanced) recasts led to a very low rate of repair. This difference suggests that context, as discussed earlier, may make a difference. It is possible that in meaning-based classroom settings, even if the teacher uses recasts with additional prompts, the learner may still take the feedback as a reaction to content rather than form. On the other hand, in more controlled dyadic interactions, it is possible that both the student and the teacher are more sensitive, and pay more attention, to feedback. Thus, students would be more likely to respond to feedback than in naturalistic classroom contexts. In addition, in the present study teachers knew in advance that they were supposed to provide feedback to learners' non-erroneous utterances. This could have affected the type of interactional feedback and the way it was provided. Therefore, before drawing any conclusions about the utility of intonationally or verbally enhanced recasts for classroom teaching, additional studies of the nature of recasts and recast enhancement in naturalistic classroom contexts are needed.

Questions and Topics for Discussion
1) What are some of the possible differences in interaction patterns between classroom interaction and non-classroom task-based interaction?
2) In recent years, a number of studies have focused on the role of recasts. What are some of the reasons that can justify this emphasis?

3) In research on the role of interaction, the term 'uptake' has been mainly used to refer to the immediate response following feedback. Allwright (1984), however, defined uptake as a term referring to what students report as having learned from a classroom lesson. Which of the two do you think would provide a better measure of the effectiveness of corrective feedback, and why?

4) Record a 5 minute interaction between a teacher and a learner. Then code the data in terms of the various kinds of corrective feedback provided. What are some of the challenges that you may face when coding the data? How can you overcome these challenges?

Notes

The study was supported by a research grant from the Social Sciences and Humanities Research Council of Canada.

References

Allwright, R. (1984). Why don't learners learn what teachers teach?: The interaction hypothesis. In D. Singleton & D. Little (Eds.), *Language learning in formal and informal contexts* (pp. 3-18). Dublin: IRAL.

Bialystok, E. (1990). The competence of processing: Classifying theories of second language acquisition. *TESOL Quarterly, 24*, 635-648.

Bialystok, E. (1994). Representation and ways of knowing: Three issues in second language acquisition. In N. Ellis (Ed.), *Explicit and implicit learning of languages* (pp. 549-569). London: Academic Press.

Braidi, S.M. (1995). Reconsidering the role of interaction and input in second language acquisition. *Language Learning, 45*, 141-175.

Braidi, S.M. (2002). Reexamining the role of recasts in native-speaker/nonnative-speaker interactions. *Language Learning, 52*, 1-42.

Carroll, S., & Swain, M. (1993). Explicit and implicit negative feedback: An empirical study of the learning of linguistic generalizations. *Studies in Second Language Acquisition, 15*, 357-386.

Chaudron, C. (1977). A descriptive model of discourse in the corrective treatment of learners' errors. *Language Learning, 27*, 29-46.

Doughty, C. (2001). Cognitive underpinning of focus on form. In P. Robinson (Ed.), *Cognition and second language instruction* (pp. 206-257). Cambridge: Cambridge University Press.

Doughty, C., & Varela, E. (1998). Communicative focus on form. In C. Doughty & J. Williams (Eds.), *Focus on form in classroom second language acquisition* (pp. 114-138). Cambridge: Cambridge University Press.

Ellis, R. (2001). *Form-focused instruction and second language learning.* Malden, MA: Blackwell Publishers.

Ellis, R., Basturkmen, H., & Loewen, S. (2001). Learner uptake in communicative ESL lessons. *Language Learning, 51,* 281-318.

Fotos, S. (1994). Integrating grammar instruction and communicative language use through grammar consciousness-raising tasks. *TESOL Quarterly, 28,* 323-351.

Fotos, S., & Ellis, R. (1991). Communicating about grammar: A task-based approach. *TESOL Quarterly, 25,* 605-628.

Gass, S., Mackey, A., & Pica, T. (1998). The role of input and interaction in second language acquisition. Introduction to the special issue. *Modern Language Journal, 82,* 299-307.

Gass, S., & Varonis, E. (1994). Input, interaction, and second language production. *Studies in Second Language Acquisition, 16,* 283-302.

Han, Z. (2002). A study of the impact of recasts on tense consistency in L2 output. *TESOL Quarterly, 36,* 543-572.

Iwashita, N. (2001). The effect of learner proficiency on interactional moves and modified output in nonnative-nonnative interaction in Japanese as a foreign language. *System, 29,* 267-287.

Iwashita, N. (2003). Negative feedback and positive evidence in task-based interaction: Differential effects on L2 development. *Studies in Second Language Acquisition, 25,* 1-36.

Leeman, J. (2003). Recasts and second language development: Beyond negative evidence. *Studies in Second Language Acquisition, 25,* 37-63.

Leow, R.P. (1997). Attention, awareness, and foreign language behavior. *Language Learning, 47,* 467-505.

Leow, R.P. (2002). Models, attention, and awareness in SLA: A response to Simard and Wong's 'Alertness, orientation, and detection: The conceptualization of attention functions in SLA.' *Studies in Second Language Acquisition, 24,* 113-119.

Long, M. (1996). The role of the linguistic environment in second language acquisition. In W. Ritchie & T. Bhatia (Eds.), *Handbook of second language acquisition* (pp. 413-468). San Diego: Academic Press.

Long, M., Inagaki, S., & Ortega, L. (1998). The role of implicit negative feedback in SLA: Models and recasts in Japanese and Spanish. *Modern Language Journal, 82,* 357-371.

Long, M., & Robinson, P. (1998). Focus on form: Theory, research, and practice. In C. Doughty & J. Williams (Eds.), *Focus on form in classroom language acquisition* (pp. 15-41). Cambridge: Cambridge University Press.

Lyster, R. (1998). Recasts, repetition, and ambiguity in L2 classroom discourse. *Studies in Second Language Acquisition, 20*, 51-81.

Lyster, R., & Ranta, L. (1997). Corrective feedback and learner uptake: Negotiation of form in communicative classrooms. *Studies in Second Language Acquisition, 19*, 37-66.

Mackey, A., Gass, S., & McDonough, K. (2000). How do learners perceive interactional feedback? *Studies in Second Language Acquisition, 22*, 471-497.

Mackey, A., & Oliver, R. (2002). Interactional feedback and children's L2 development. *System, 30*, 459-477.

Mackey, A., Oliver, R., & Leeman, J. (2003). Interactional input and the incorporation of feedback: An exploration of NS-NNS and NNS-NNS adult and child dyads. *Language Learning, 53*, 35-66.

Mackey, A., & Philp, J. (1998). Conversational interaction and second language development: Recasts, responses, and red herrings? *Modern Language Journal, 82*, 338-356.

McDonough, K. (2005). Identifying the impact of negative feedback and learners' responses on ESL question development. *Studies in Second Language Acquisition, 27*, 79-103.

McDonough, K., & Mackey, A. (2000). Communicative tasks, conversational interaction and linguistic form: An empirical study of Thai. *Foreign Language Annals, 33*, 82-92.

Morris, F.A., & Tarone, E.E. (2003). Impact of classroom dynamics on the effectiveness of recasts in second language acquisition. *Language Learning, 53*, 325-368.

Nassaji, H. (1999). Towards integrating form-focused instruction and communicative interaction in the second language classroom: Some pedagogical possibilities. *Canadian Modern Language Review, 55*, 385-402.

Nassaji, H., & Fotos, S. (2004). Current developments in research on the teaching of grammar. *Annual Review of Applied Linguistics, 24*, 126-145.

Nassaji, H., & Wells, G. (2000). What's the use of 'triadic dialogue'?: An investigation of teacher-student interaction. *Applied Linguistics, 21*, 376-406.

Oliver, R. (2000). Age differences in negotiation and feedback in classroom and pairwork. *Language Learning, 50*, 119-151.

Oliver, R., & Mackey, A. (2003). Interactional context and feedback in child ESL classrooms. *Modern Language Journal, 87*, 519-533.

Panova, I., & Lyster, R. (2002). Patterns of corrective feedback and uptake in an adult ESL classroom. *TESOL Quarterly, 36*, 573-595.

Pica, T. (1994). Research on negotiation: What does it reveal about L2 learning conditions, processes, and outcomes. *Language Learning, 44*, 493-527.

Pica, T. (1996). Do second language learners need negotiation? *IRAL-International Review of Applied Linguistics in Language Teaching, 34,* 1-21.

Pica, T. (2002). Subject-matter content: How does it assist the interactional and linguistic needs of classroom language learners? *Modern Language Journal, 86,* 1-19.

Robinson, P. (1995). Attention, memory, and the noticing hypothesis. *Language Learning, 45,* 283-331.

Schmidt, R. (1993). Awareness and second language acquisition. *Annual Review of Applied Linguistics, 13,* 206-226.

Schmidt, R. (1995). Consciousness and foreign language learning: A tutorial on the role of attention and awareness in language learning. In R. Schmidt (Ed.), *Attention and awareness in foreign language learning* (pp. 1-63). Honolulu: University of Hawai'i Press.

Schmidt, R. (2001). Attention. In P. Robinson (Ed.), *Cognition and second language instruction* (pp. 3-32). Cambridge: Cambridge University Press.

Sharwood Smith, M. (1993). Input enhancement in instructed SLA. *Studies in Second Language Acquisition, 15,* 165-179.

Tomlin, R., & Villa, V. (1994). Attention in cognitive science and second language acquisition. *Studies in Second Language Acquisition, 16,* 183-202.

VanPatten, B. (2002). Processing the content of input-processing and processing instruction research: A response to DeKeyser, Salaberry, Robinson, and Harrington. *Language Learning, 52,* 825-831.

Chapter 5
Saliency in Second Language Listening and Reading

Mark H. Overstreet, Dickinson College

There are not many aspects of theory that all second language acquisition (SLA) researchers can agree on. If there is one, it is that input is absolutely necessary for second language acquisition to occur. Learners must be exposed to the language they are learning in meaningful, communicatively-driven contexts that allow them to make the form–meaning connections necessary for building an internal linguistic system.

An essential question, then, is how do learners select the language that they attend to in the input? Humans are limited capacity cognitive processors; they can only process so much information, in this case linguistic information, at one time. Learners must select, whether consciously or unconsciously, the linguistic information to which they pay attention. By applying attentional resources to a subset of the input learners are able to process it more efficiently for meaning.

Factors that influence what is salient are both external to the learner, having to do with features of the language, and internal to the learner, having to do with the distribution of attentional resources. The goal of this chapter is to review various characteristics of input to demonstrate the features that make linguistic items salient to learners in both aural and written environments. The chapter begins with a brief discussion of the role of attention and how salience may affect the distribution of attentional resources. Next, I review a set of Operating Principles for listening comprehension. Third, I review a theory of saliency in reading, based primarily on first language reading research. Fourth, I discuss textual enhancement research in second language acquisition. Finally, the chapter concludes with a discussion of the next step, that is what learners do with language that is salient.

The Role of Attention

At any given point in time throughout the day, our senses are bombarded by a variety of stimuli. We see, we hear, we touch, we smell, we taste constantly. However, we are seldom overwhelmed by the sheer volume of stimuli because our brain is designed to filter out, not to eliminate but to push to the background, those stimuli that are not most salient for our current situation. For example, while driving, we have to process an array of auditory information. There is the music on the radio, the conversation we are having with a passenger, the sound of the car on the road itself, and the sounds of other vehicles as they pass us (or we pass them). Which of these sounds is most salient? For most people, the answer will probably be the voice of their passenger. The volume of this voice doesn't drown out the radio, but it is the most salient because we attend to what our passenger is saying. When, suddenly, another driver blows a horn next to or behind us, our attention shifts due to volume, surprise, and the knowledge that the horn may be trying to communicate a potentially urgent situation. Because of volume and immediacy, the horn becomes the most salient.

This simple explanation gives insight into the nature of human attention: It is limited, it is selective, and it is controllable. It is limited in the sense that we cannot attend to all stimuli equally, such as all of the sounds that assail us while driving. It is selective, meaning that it will reduce the impact of some stimuli, such as the sound of the radio, and focus on other stimuli, the sound of the passenger's voice. Finally, it is controllable in that we can choose which stimuli we attend to. If I prefer the music on the radio to my three-year-old's story about Elmo, I can control my attention to attend to the lyrics of the songs. Moreover, if a more salient sound occurs, such as a car horn, I can shift all of my attention to that sound or to other stimuli that will help me analyze the situation (see Schmidt, 2001 for a detailed review of the aspects of attention).

The task of language learners is like that of the driver in that there is a lot of "noise" that occurs as they attend to input (whether in aural or written form), and they must determine what is most useful to attend to in order to make the form–meaning connections that will help them comprehend the message and develop their linguistic systems. At different moments and at different levels of proficiency, attention must be paid to some items, and no attention need be given to others, for comprehension to occur. Indeed, the role of attention is so important for Slobin (1985) that it is the very first of his Operating Principles (OPs) for language processing: "OP (ATTENTION): Sounds. Store any perceptually salient stretches of speech" (p. 1165).

Saliency in Listening Comprehension

Klein (1986) identified a series of four tasks that a listener must complete in order to comprehend an input stream: analysis, synthesis, embedding, and matching. In this section, the focus will be on what Klein calls the problem of **analysis**, that is, the challenge, especially for an early language learner, of finding words and word boundaries in a speech stream. For Klein, the first task facing the learner is to separate words so that they can be processed for meaning. Until word boundaries and words are identified, a speech stream is nothing more than a series of sounds. For instance, think about the first time you heard a new language. It probably sounded considerably faster than your native language, the sounds likely did not make sense, and there was no clear break between the words you heard. As you gained experience with the language, you started to pick out individual sounds and words, and you were eventually able to piece together meaning. The question before us in this section is what factors of the speech stream itself influence its analysis and, eventually, allow you to move on to the next step, that of assigning meaning to the words you have analyzed.

Peters (1985) identifies this step as the initial **extraction problem** and defines it as "the process of recognizing and remembering chunks of speech out of the continuous speech streams present in the environment" (p. 1030). Peters established a set of Operating Principles that children use to analyze incoming speech streams in their first language. Once learners extract pieces of language, they must then segment them into meaningful units, such as words and morphological markings that can then be assigned meaning. Peters' first three OPs deal with the problem of extraction, that is, how listeners extract and store linguistic information:

> EX: EXTRACT. Extract whatever salient chunks of speech you can.
> EX: COMPARE. Determine whether a newly extracted chunk of speech seems to be the same as or different from anything you have already stored.
> EX: STORE. If it is different, then store it separately; if it is the same, take note of this sameness but do not store it separately (p. 1033).

She also proposes a series of OPs based on the phonological structure of the speech stream that may make some portions of the stream more salient than others:

> EX: SILENCE. An extractable unit is bounded by silence (i.e., it is a whole utterance).
> EX: SUPRASEG. An extractable unit is a suprasegmentally delimited stretch of speech.
> EX: TUNE. An extractable unit is a speech tune or melody.
> EX: RHYTHM. An extractable unit is a rhythmic pattern of speech (p. 1034).

An example of a suprasegmentally delimited stretch of speech might be a comprehension check question, "you know?" "you think?" or a clarification question "isn't it?" that is tagged onto the end of a longer speech stream. An example of a tune unit might include words such as "uh-oh" in English, which has a distinctive sing-song pattern.

Once the units are extracted, learners have to segment them, or parse them into smaller linguistic units that carry meaning. These may be groups of words, words, or parts of words. The guiding Operating Principle is:

> SG: SEGMENT. Attempt to segment utterances you hear or utterances you have already extracted into smaller linguistic units (p. 1037).

The phonological cues used for segmenting a speech stream are subsections of this OP and assume that learners are able to segment an extracted unit into syllables.

> SG: INTONATION. Segment utterances at intonationally salient places.

SG: RHYTHM. Segment utterances at rhythmically salient places.
SG: STRESS. Segment off a stressed syllable of an extracted unit and store it separately.
SG: END. Segment off the last syllable of an extracted unit and store it separately.
SG: BEGIN. Segment off the first syllable of an extracted unit and store it separately.
SG: REPETITION. Segment off subunits that are repeated (in terms of segments, rhythm, or intonation) within an extracted unit and store them separately (p. 1038).

Slobin (1985) takes Peters' (1985) SEGMENT Operating Principles and combines them within an overall ATTENTION OP:

OP (ATTENTION): END OF UNIT. Pay attention to the last syllable of an extracted speech unit. Store it separately and also in relation to the unit with which it occurs.
OP (ATTENTION): BEGINNING OF UNIT. Pay attention to the first syllable of an extracted speech unit. Store it separately and also in relation to the unit with which it occurs.
OP (ATTENTION): STRESS. Pay attention to the stressed syllables in extracted speech units. Store such syllables separately and also in relation to the units with which they occur (p. 1166).

Slobin changes the focus from the actual mental processes of extraction or segmentation. Instead, he stresses the importance of where in the speech stream one should pay attention so that an effective and efficient extraction or segmentation is achieved. If listeners pay attention, whether consciously or unconsciously, to specific portions of a speech stream to gain linguistic information, then this may be an indication of how teachers can adjust speech streams in order to increase the likelihood that students will attend to the targeted elements.

Both Peters (1985) and Slobin (1985) examined the Operating Principles that children use while learning their first language. Klein (1986), however, specifically looked at second language acquisition and found that many of the processes of initial analysis are similar, if not identical, to those recognized in first language acquisition.

Like Peters (1985) and Slobin (1985), Klein (1986) places importance on location within an utterance. According to Klein, processing priority has the following order: "the opening segment(s) of an utterance, the concluding segment(s), [and] the segment(s) immediately preceding and following any identifiable pauses" (p. 68). His argument is that the change from sound to silence and from silence to sound is salient, and therefore will cause listeners to attend more carefully to the information at those borders. This argument parallels Peters' EX: SILENCE.

The proposals set forth by Peters (1985), Slobin (1985), and Klein (1986) suggest a model of processing that is serial in nature. As a speech stream begins, the learner will begin processing immediately and attempt to process the stream in order. This means that the processing resources will at some point be overwhelmed as the learner hears more and is unable to process the entire stream. When the stream ends, the latter portions of the utterance may remain in memory long enough for the learner to process them. As learners gain proficiency in their second language (L2), and are able to process an input stream more effectively, they will be able to process more from both the beginning and the end, which will eventually allow them to begin processing middle portions of the speech stream.

Klein also argues that intonation, or prosody, plays a role in salience. The prosodic features he notes are loudness, pitch, duration of segments, intonation, stress, and rhythm (p. 69). These features, Klein argues, will draw attention to words that are most important from a communicative standpoint. He states that "stress explains to some extent why content words are usually acquired more easily than function words, even though the latter are much more frequent" (p. 70). Although function words occur more frequently, content words (i.e., nouns and verbs) are more likely to be stressed, and therefore will be more salient. Once again, Klein's proposals parallel the OPs set forth by Peters and Slobin. The two factors on which all three researchers place the most emphasis are location of an item within an utterance and stress.

There are relatively few recent studies in SLA research that have examined these factors and their affect on saliency for listeners/learners. Kim (1995), however, sought to determine which elements of speech L2 listeners attend to, what the phonological characteristics of that speech are, and whether or not the characteristics can be placed into a developmental pattern. Kim's 26 first language Korean speakers learning English listened to a total of thirty passages that were 3-6 clauses in length. The participants' comprehension was measured by having them select the appropriate picture from a set of options for each passage. Immediately after making a selection, participants had to reveal how they made their choice. There were no differences on the comprehension measure, but several patterns emerged concerning the noticing of elements in the passages. The first was that elements that carried stress were noticed most often. The next most frequently reported elements were those located in either an initial or a final position.

Barcroft and VanPatten (1997) conducted a study to answer the following research questions: 1) Does location within an utterance in the L2 affect the perceptibility of certain grammatical forms for learners? If so, which of the three locations, utterance-initial, utterance-medial, or utterance-final, is the most salient? 2) Does the presence of stress affect the perceptibility of grammatical forms? 3) Does the boundedness of a grammatical item have an effect? (In Spanish, verbal conjugation morphemes, such as *–aba*, are bounded at the end of verbs. Object pronouns, such as *lo, le*, are unbounded morphemes that precede verbs.) Their 18 subjects listened to the target sentences in a quiet room. After hearing each sentence, participants repeated aloud what they had heard. Barcroft and VanPatten found a main effect for sentence position, as more words from the initial position were repeated correctly compared to those in medial or final positions. They also found that stressed items were repeated more often than unstressed items. They found no main effect for the boundedness of the morphemes. Finally, in all cases, they found no difference between the medial and final positions. Barcroft and VanPatten concluded that learners do not start off with the initial>final>medial processing strategy. Instead, they process only sentence initial information. The ability to process other information may come later as learners develop proficiency in the language.

Rosa and O'Neill (1998) conducted a partial replication of Barcroft and VanPatten (1997). They asked the following research questions: Does location within an utterance in an L2 affect how linguistic forms are perceived? If so, which location is the most salient? And, does stress affect the saliency of target linguistic items? (p. 32). Rosa and O'Neill used the stressed *sé* and unstressed *se,* and the stressed *-ó* and unstressed *–o* as their targets in initial, medial, and final positions. Participants listened to 18 sentences in one of ten random orders. Twelve of the sentences contained the target items and six were distractor sentences. Immediately after hearing a sentence, participants had to repeat it aloud. Rosa and O'Neill's results showed a main effect for both location and stress with *sé/se*. Overall, the stressed *sé* was more salient than the unstressed *se*. For both *sé* and *se* the initial position was more salient than the other positions. For *sé* the final position was not more salient than the medial position, but for *se* it was. The results showed a main effect for location and a significant interaction between stress and location for –ó/-o. In this case, the stressed –ó was not more salient than the unstressed –o. Instead, the interaction was the result of the initial stressed –ó being more salient than the other positions, and the final –ó being more salient than the medial position. For the unstressed –o, the initial position was not more salient than the medial position, but the final position was more salient than the medial position. Rosa and O'Neill concluded that the most salient position is the initial position, and the most salient combination is the stressed initial position. However, they categorized their findings more like those of Kim (1995) than those of Barcroft and VanPatten (1997) because they found significant differences between the utterance final and utterance medial positions.

Rast and Dommergues (2003) conducted a study to find out what is salient to learners during initial exposure to a new language and what, if anything, changes after minimal exposure to the language. Their subjects were eight monolingual French learners who had no previous exposure to Polish. Rast and Dommergues made three predictions about the saliency of words in an utterance based on the structure of the utterance itself:

- stressed words will be more salient than unstressed words;
- words with sounds closer to the native language will be repeated better than words with novel sounds, what they termed "phonemic distance" (p. 136);
- words at the beginning will be more salient than those at the end, and those at the end will be more salient than those in the middle.

Participants were tested by listening to a recording of a Polish speaker reading 17 sentences and then repeating what they heard out loud. Participants received a point if a native speaker of Polish determined that the repeated word had the same number of syllables as the original word and if there was a maximum of one incorrectly repeated phoneme. Testing took place on three occasions: before any exposure to Polish, after four hours of exposure, and after eight hours of exposure.

Rast and Dommergues' results show a main effect for amount of instruction in all cases; that is with more exposure, participants were able to repeat more syllables correctly. They found a main effect for stress as hypothesized; stressed words were repeated more correctly than unstressed words for all three time periods. They also found a main effect for phonemic distance for all three periods. Finally, they found a main effect for word location; that is initial and final words were pronounced with the same level of correctness, while words in medial positions were repeated less correctly.

Rast and Dommergues also made predictions about other characteristics of the input that they believed would influence saliency. They predicted that two syllable words would be repeated more correctly than either one syllable words or multisyllable words. They also predicted that words that had more transparent meanings (how close the word meaning in the L2 is to the L1) would be repeated correctly more often. Finally, they predicted that words that occurred frequently in the input would be repeated correctly more often.

Their results showed that there was no effect for word length on correct repetitions. Words from 1-6 syllables were repeated correctly at the same rate. However, they did find an effect for transparency of meaning. Words that were determined to be very or fairly transparent were repeated more correctly than words that were not transparent. They also found a main effect for the frequency of words in the input after eight hours of instruction. Words that occurred frequently were repeated more correctly than words that were rare or not in the input.

Rast and Dommergues found interactions between word location and other variables that give important insight into learners' listening strategies. They found that correct repetition of short words in initial position was very successful, while correct repetition of short words in final position was less so. On the contrary, correct repetition of long words in initial position was very low, yet it was much higher in final position. For words of all lengths, the middle position demonstrated the lowest level of correct repetition. Finally, phonemic distance showed effects in initial and final positions only. Rast and Dommergues concluded that, for learners with minimal experience with an L2, the most salient words are those in initial position, those that are stressed, those that are similar sounding to words in the L1, those that have more obvious meanings, and those that occur frequently.

This review shows that, as Peters (1985) and Slobin (1985) observed in first language acquisition, and as Klein (1986) proposed for second language acquisition, sentence position and stress are two key factors in making a particular item in the input stream salient to learners. Klein's problem of analysis, then, can most easily be solved by taking this into account when making a prediction about whether or not target items will be salient to learners in naturalistic input. If they are not salient, then steps may need to be taken for learners to be able to attend to them.

Auditory Saliency in the Classroom

The studies reviewed above found that the initial position and stressed words tend to be salient for learners. In addition, Rast and Dommergues went on to determine other factors that make words more salient for beginning L2 learners. This knowledge can be of use to classroom teachers to help identify those items that will need some sort of manipulation when they are the object of study. For instance, items that normally occur in the middle of sentences, such as the subjunctive in Spanish, will naturally be less salient to learners. However, instructors can manipulate exercises to make the target more salient. For example, a typical Spanish sentence with the subjunctive in a noun clause looks like the following: *El profesor quiere que los estudiantes estudien mucho antes de los exámenes.* The target subjunctive morphology *–en* of *estudien* is both unstressed and medial, placing it in the least salient position. The instructor could construct an activity that moves the target to the beginning of the sentence during a listening exercise. Learners might hear the dependent clause ...*que estudien mucho antes de los exámenes* and have to select one of two independent clauses *El profesor quiere...* and *El profesor sabe...* one of which takes the subjunctive and the other does not. In this way, the target form is more salient because of its location in the utterance, and, in addition, learners have to make the form-meaning connection between the target form and the target meaning.

Another strategy is to stress words that may not be stressed in ordinary discourse to intentionally render them salient. Another example from Spanish, and drawing on Barcroft and VanPatten (1997), is to stress pronouns orally even if they do not normally receive such stress: *No quiero estudiarlo hoy.* In French, the dual negative marker *ne...pas* is unstressed, and the first element is nearly elided by some speakers. That element, or both, could be stressed: *Je ne vais pas étudier.*

VanPatten (1990), however, demonstrated that we must be cautious when attempting to manipulate learners' attention during listening. In his study, learners were asked to listen to a passage in Spanish in one of four experimental groups: the first group listened for content only; the second group listened for content plus the vocabulary word *inflación*; the third group listened for content plus the article *la*; the fourth group listened for content plus the verbal morphology *–n*. VanPatten found that across three levels of learners, listening for grammatical items reduced the amount of passage information that participants were able to recall. He concluded that conscious attention to form and conscious attention to meaning compete for resources, and that drawing attention to form may detract from comprehending propositional content.

Saliency during Reading

Reading comprehension does not pose the same inherent challenges for learners that listening comprehension does. During listening comprehension, learners are faced with the challenge of parsing sentences into words before they can make sense of them. As Klein (1985) pointed out, one of the first tasks is that of analysis. To complete analysis, learners depend on salient items in a speech stream to locate words and word boundaries. In addition, a speech stream must be comprehended in real time, with no opportunity to go back and repeat, unless the listener requests it. In listening comprehension saliency plays a role in the analysis and comprehension of the speech stream, in reading we will see that it plays a role in comprehension and recall of text content.

A written text provides both the word boundaries and the opportunity to go back and reread as many times as a person desires. It might seem, therefore, that all words in a text are equally salient to the reader. The research shows, however, that in reading, there is a direct link between visual saliency and recall. Lorch (1989) reviewed an array of research on the use of text-signaling devices and reached two general conclusions. First, that textual enhancement has a positive effect on memory for the signaled content, and second that drawing extra attention to some items has either no effect on recall of other content, or has a negative effect (p. 224).

In first language reading research a number of studies have demonstrated that text that has been manipulated in some way, either through bolding, italics, or other textual enhancements, is recalled more successfully than text that is not. Textbooks rely on these techniques to signal important concepts, terms, and other content items so that students will be more likely to notice them and, therefore, able to recall them. Lorch (1989) determined that textual enhancement is only effective if the relationship between the signaled content and the cue is obvious to learners.

There is, however, a ceiling for the positive effects of textual enhancement in first language reading. Lorch, Lorch Pugzles, and Klusewitz (1995) completed a study using a brief text in three conditions: no highlighting, light highlighting, and heavy highlighting. Their results showed no difference between the no highlighting and heavy highlighting conditions on a cued recall task. They concluded that the use of heavy highlighting essentially overwhelmed the readers and did not allow them to focus on content as much as the light highlighting.

In first language acquisition, therefore, the role of textual enhancement has been well established as a manner of increasing comprehension and recall of a text. In second language acquisition research textual enhancement has been seen as a means of drawing attention not to the content of a text, but rather to particular grammatical forms in order to signal them for increased attention and additional processing. Unfortunately, results in this line of research are inconclusive. Whereas Alanen (1995) and Shook (1994) found positive effects for textual enhancement on the acquisition of target items, Jourdenais (1998), Leow (1997), Overstreet (1998, 2000), and Wong (2000) found no effect for enhancement on acquisition.

Wong (2000) conducted a study in French to determine the effects of textual enhancement on the acquisition of a grammatical item of no communicative value: past participle agreement in relative clauses. Her participants read texts in French in one of four conditions: simplified with textual enhancement, unsimplified with textual enhancement, simplified without textual enhancement, unsimplified without textual enhancement. She found that textual enhancement did not have any effect based on an error correction task, but she did find that learners recalled the target sentences as a whole when they were enhanced. This finding reflects first language reading research.

Jourdenais et al. (1995) conducted a study in Spanish on the effect of textual enhancement on the acquisition of the preterit and imperfect. Their participants read a Spanish version of Little Red Riding Hood in either unenhanced or enhanced texts. They then completed a story-writing task based on a series of pictures. While completing the story writing task, participants had to say aloud what they were thinking. The researchers found that those participants who read the text with enhancement mentioned the use of the preterit and imperfect more often as they were writing and used the preterit and imperfect more as they wrote. However, there was no difference in accuracy between the two groups. The researchers concluded that the enhancement made participants more aware of the past tense and, therefore, primed them to use it more often. These two studies show that increasing perceptual salience through textual enhancement does have an effect on learners similar to that noted in first language reading.

Overstreet (2002) studied the effects of textual enhancement on reading comprehension and form recognition. His third-semester Spanish participants read a text about the Mayan civilization in one of five experimental treatments: no enhancement, enhancement of progressive morphology, enhancement of the entire progressive verb, enhancement of imperfect subjunctive morphology, and enhancement of the entire imperfect subjunctive verb. After participants finished the reading, they completed a free recall task in English and a form recognition task in Spanish. The form recognition task required participants to pick out the form of the verb that appeared in the reading from five choices. The results showed that there was no difference between enhancing just the morphology or enhancing the entire verb. There was a positive correlation between recall of the target sentence and the enhanced progressive verb, and a negative correlation between recall of the target sentence and the enhanced imperfect subjunctive verb. In other words, with the progressive, the better the learners recalled the sentence context in which the verb appeared, the better they recalled the verb itself, and vice versa. With the subjunctive, if learners recalled the sentence context, they did not recall the verb, and vice versa. Overstreet concluded that for early-acquired grammatical items, like the progressive, enhancement has an enabling effect for both form and content. For late-acquired grammatical items, that is items that were likely not yet in the linguistic systems of his participants, Overstreet concluded that there was a trade off in attention and therefore learners had to choose either one or the other, form or content.

What Comes after Perceptual Saliency?

As Klein (1985) noted, the analysis of a speech stream, or text sentence, is only the first step toward comprehension and language acquisition. What learners do with the information they are able to parse from the input source requires a completely different set of processes that rely on the fact that learners have found the words and the word boundaries and are working hard to comprehend the incoming message. This set of processes is called input processing and focuses on how words and parts of words are processed together by a listener/reader to comprehend an input stream.

VanPatten (1996, 2004) proposed one of the dominant models of input processing. VanPatten's model was developed to describe the manner in which learners process auditory, rather than written, input. Although there is some research to suggest that the model may have some application in the written mode (e.g., Greenslade, Bouden, & Sanz, 1999; Overstreet, 2002; Wong, 2001), more research needs to be done to determine the similarities and differences between the auditory and written modes.

VanPatten's (2004) first principle is the Primacy of Meaning Principle. That is, learners will process input for meaning before they process it for form (p. 14). This principle breaks with the idea of a serial processing model because it predicts that learners will look for content words, such as nouns and verbs, rather than simply process text in a serial manner. However, VanPatten also includes a Sentence Location Principle as part of his model because of the perceptual saliency of certain utterance locations. For example, a content word in initial position will be processed before one in final position.

Conclusions

Language learning is not one simple process from beginning to end. As we learn a new language, our first task is to separate all of the sounds we hear into words. The central goal of this chapter was to discuss the characteristics of a spoken input stream that assist learners in making that analysis. As with first language learning, the factors that are most important in making portions of the input salient (whether they are groups of words, words, or parts of words) are the location of the element in the input stream and the stress the element receives.

In the written mode, the task of separating words has been completed for the reader, but that does not mean that the problem is solved. Learners must still assign meaning to the elements in the input, and there remains a competition between paying attention to meaning and paying attention to form. Instructors can use this information to manipulate input, in either mode, to allow learners to apply their attention where it will be most effective for language learning. However, using such techniques should always be done keeping the importance of comprehension in mind. Making an item salient without giving the learner an opportunity to apply meaning to it will not be successful. On the other hand, if instructors make items more salient in communicative contexts that allow learners to make form–meaning connections more successfully, learners may acquire language more quickly and effectively.

Questions and Topics for Discussion

1) What is the problem of *analysis* (Klein, 1986) and how does salience aid in solving it?
2) What does it mean to say that we are more likely to attend to more salient items than to less salient items?
3) In the following example sentence, *Bob decided to ask Evelyn to send a letter to Paul*, who will tend to be the most salient actor? The second most salient? Why? Which action will tend to be the most salient? How might a beginning language learner who has difficulty parsing very much language hear the sentence?
4) On the written page, all items are equally salient. Explain why you agree or disagree with this statement.

References

Alanen, R. (1995). Input enhancement and rule presentation in second language acquisition. In R. Schmidt (Ed.), *Attention and awareness in foreign language learning* (pp. 183-216). Honolulu: University of Hawai'i Press.

Barcroft, J., & VanPatten, B. (1997). Acoustic salience of grammatical forms: The effect of location, stress, and boundedness on Spanish L2 input processing. In A.T. Pérez-Leroux & W. Glass (Eds.), *Contemporary perspectives on the acquisition of Spanish. Vol. 2: Production, processing, and comprehension* (pp. 109-121). Somerville, MA: Cascadilla Press.

Greenslade, T., Bouden, L., & Sanz, C. (1999). Attending to form and content in processing L2 reading texts. *Spanish Applied Linguistics, 3,* 65-90.

Jourdenais, R. (1998). *The effects of textual enhancement on the acquisition of the Spanish preterit and imperfect.* Unpublished doctoral dissertation, Georgetown University.

Jourdenais, R., Ota, M., Stauffer, S., Boyson, B., & Doughty, C. (1995). Does textual enhancement promote noticing? A think-aloud protocol analysis. In R. Schmidt (Ed.), *Attention and awareness in foreign language learning* (pp. 183-216). Honolulu: University of Hawai'i Press.

Kim, H-Y. (1995). Intake from the speech stream: Speech elements that L2 learners attend to. In R. Schmidt (Ed.), *Attention and awareness in foreign language learning* (pp. 183-216). Honolulu: University of Hawai'i Press.

Klein, W. (1986). *Second language acquisition*. Cambridge: Cambridge University Press.

Leow, R. (1997). The effects of input enhancement and text length on adult L2 readers' comprehension and intake in second language acquisition. *Applied Language Learning, 8,* 151-182.

Lorch, Jr., R. (1989). Text-signaling devices and their effects on reading and memory processes. *Educational Psychology Review, 1,* 209-234.

Lorch Jr., R., Pugzles Lorch, E., & Klusewitz, M. (1995). Effects of typographical cues on reading and recall of text. *Contemporary Educational Psychology, 20,* 51-64.

Overstreet, M. (1998). Text enhancement and content familiarity: The focus of learner attention. *Spanish Applied Linguistics, 2,* 229-258.

Overstreet, M. (2000, March). *Textual enhancement over time: Effects on comprehension, intake and production.* Paper presented at the meeting of the American Association for Applied Linguistics, Vancouver, BC, Canada.

Overstreet, M. (2002). *The effect of textual enhancement on second language learner reading comprehension and form recognition.* Unpublished doctoral dissertation, University of Illinois at Urbana-Champaign.

Peters, A. (1985). Language segmentation: Operating principles for the perception and analysis of language. In D. Slobin (Ed.), *Crosslinguistic study of language acquisition, Vol. 2: Theoretical issues* (pp. 1157-1249). Hillsdale, NJ: Lawrence Erlbaum.

Rast, R., & Dommergues, J-Y. (2003). Towards a characterisation of saliency on first exposure to a second language. *EUROSLA Yearbook, 3,* 131-156.

Rosa, E., & O'Neill, M. (1998). Effects of stress and location on acoustic salience at the initial stages of Spanish L2 input processing. *Spanish Applied Linguistics, 2,* 24-52.

Schmidt, R. (2001). Attention. In P. Robinson (Ed.), *Cognition and second language instruction* (pp. 3-32). Cambridge: Cambridge University Press.

Shook, D. (1994). FL/L2 Reading, grammatical information, and the input-to-intake phenomenon. *Applied Language Learning, 5,* 57-93.

Slobin, D. (1985). Crosslinguistic evidence for the language-making capacity. In D. Slobin (Ed.), *Crosslinguistic study of language acquisition, Vol. 2: Theoretical issues* (pp. 1157-1249). Hillsdale, NJ: Lawrence Erlbaum.

VanPatten, B. (1990). Attending to form and content in the input: An experiment in consciousness. *Studies in Second Language Acquisition, 12,* 287-301.

VanPatten, B. (1996). *Input processing and grammar instruction.* Norwood, NJ: Ablex.

VanPatten, B. (2004). Input processing in second language acquisition. In B. VanPatten (Ed.), *Processing instruction: Theory, research, and commentary* (pp. 5-31). Mahwah, NJ: Lawrence Erlbaum.

Wong, W. (2000). *The effects of textual enhancement and simplified input on L2 comprehension and acquisition of non-meaningful grammatical form.* Unpublished doctoral dissertation, University of Illinois at Urbana-Champaign.

Wong, W. (2001). Modality and attention to meaning and form in the input. *Studies in Second Language Acquisition, 23,* 345-368.

Chapter 6
Processing Instruction and Structured Input as Input Enhancement

Wynne Wong, Ohio State University

Processing instruction (PI), as an input enhancement technique, is a type of pedagogical intervention that is informed by the strategies that second language (L2) learners use to make form-meaning connections as they try to comprehend aural or written L2 input. These strategies are delineated in VanPatten's model of input processing (VanPatten, 1993, 1996, 2002, 2004). The goal of PI is to help L2 learners derive richer intake from input by having them engage in structured input (SI) activities that are designed to pull them away from inefficient processing strategies toward more optimal ones. This chapter will describe in detail the nature of PI, focusing on SI activities, as an input enhancement technique and how this technique serves to make target forms more salient so that L2 learners are pushed to notice and process these forms. Included in the chapter are guidelines for the creation of SI activities as well as a brief discussion of research that supports the use of PI and SI activities as an input enhancement tool in the classroom.

VanPatten's Model of Input Processing

Because PI is informed by a model of how L2 learners initially process L2 input to make form-meaning connections, that is to say, VanPatten's model of input processing, it would be useful to begin here. VanPatten conceptualizes second language acquisition (SLA) as the result of internal mechanisms, consisting of a set of processes, which act on meaning-bearing input (Wong, 2004a). The first process, known as input processing, involves the conversion of input into intake. **Intake,** used in this sense, refers to input that L2 learners pay attention to and from which form-meaning connections have been made (VanPatten, 1996). This subsequent processing involves the partial or complete incorporation, or **accommodation,** of data into the system. Depending on the nature of the data, accommodation may have an effect on the developing system such that some kind of restructuring may occur. Finally, linguistic data that have been incorporated into the developing system may be eventually accessed by the learner as output. This process is called **access**.

VanPatten's model of input processing focuses on the first process. It contains a set of principles and subprinciples (see Table 6.1) to explain (1) what learners attend to in the input and why, (2) what strategies

Table 6.1: Principles of VanPatten's Model of Input Processing

---

Principle 1 (P1). The Primacy of Meaning Principle. Learners process input for meaning before they process it for form.
P1a. The Primacy of Content Words Principle. Learners process content words in the input before anything else.
P1b. The Lexical Preference Principle. Learners will tend to rely on lexical items as opposed to grammatical form to get meaning when both encode the same semantic information.
P1c. The Preference for Nonredundancy Principle. Learners are more likely to process nonredundant meaningful grammatical forms before they process redundant meaningful forms.
P1d. The Meaning-before-Nonmeaning Principle. Learners are more likely to process meaningful grammatical forms before nonmeaningful forms irrespective of redundancy.
P1e. The Availability of Resources Principle. For learners to process either redundant meaningful grammatical forms or nonmeaningful forms, the processing of overall sentential meaning must not drain available processing resources.
P1f. The Sentence Location Principle. Learners tend to process items in sentence initial position before those in final position and those in medial position.
Principle 2 (P2). The First Noun Principle. Learners tend to process the first noun or pronoun they encounter in a sentence as the subject or agent.
P2a. The Lexical Semantics Principle. Learners may rely on lexical semantics, where possible, instead of word order to interpret sentences.
P2b. The Event Probabilities Principle. Learners may rely on event probabilities, where possible, instead of word order to interpret sentences.
P2c. The Contextual Constraint Principle. Learners may rely less on the First Noun Principle if preceding context constrains the possible interpretation of a clause or sentence.

Source: VanPatten (2004)

guide how they make form-meaning connections, and (3) why they make some form-meaning connections before others.

Principle 1

The first principle and subprinciples of the model are based on an understanding that when learners are exposed to L2 input, they are driven to retrieve meaning first (Principle 1). In other words, learners will try to understand the message the input coveys before paying attention to how that message is encoded linguistically. This means that more meaningful items in the input will initially get processed before less meaningful ones and implies that content words are probably the first items that learners process (see P1a) (e.g., see research by Musumeci, 1989; Lee, Cadierno, Glass, & VanPatten, 1997). The subprinciples go on to explain that if a lexical item and a grammatical form both encode the same semantic information, the learner will process the lexical item before the grammatical form (see P1b). Consider the following sentence:

1) Yesterday evening Carol cooked dinner.

Temporal reference in this sentence is encoded in two ways: the content lexical items *yesterday evening* and the morphological form *-ed* of the verb *cook*. According to Principle 1, if learners wanted to determine the temporal reference of the above sentence, they would pay attention to or process the content lexical items *yesterday evening* before the morphological form *-ed* in the verb *cook* because the content lexical items carry more meaning.

An important construct in understanding the first principle of VanPatten's model is the concept of communicative value. **Communicative value** refers to the meaning that a form contributes to overall meaning in a stream of input and is based on two features: +/- inherent semantic value and +/- redundancy (Wong, 2005). A form that has **inherent semantic value** is a form that has some kind of meaning built into the form. Going back to the sample sentence discussed earlier, we could say that the *–ed* of the verb *cooked* has inherent semantic value because it expresses the meaning of pastness. An example of a form that does not have inherent semantic value is the third person singular *–s* as in *she speaks*. The *–s* does not have inherent semantic value because it does not express any meaning.

Redundancy refers to whether the information carried in the form is also expressed elsewhere in a sentence or utterance. For example, in the sentence we looked at earlier, the form *–ed* in the verb *cooked* is redundant because it encodes the meaning of pastness and pastness is already expressed by the content words *yesterday evening*.

Any given form can have +semantic value and – redundancy, + semantic value and + redundancy, – semantic value and + redundancy, and – semantic value and – redundancy. The communicative value of a form is higher if it has the characteristics + semantic value and – redundancy than if it had the features + semantic value and + redundancy. The reason for this is because if the referential meaning of a piece of input can be derived from something other than from the form in question, then the communicative value of that form would be diminished. In (1), the communicative value of the form *–ed* is diminished because we can get the concept of pastness (which the *–ed* encodes) from the content words *yesterday evening*. However, watch what happens when we remove *yesterday evening* from the input.

2) Carol cooked dinner.

By removing the content words *yesterday evening* from the sentence, we have increased the communicative value of *–ed* because learners can no longer rely on *yesterday evening* to get temporal reference. They now have no choice but to rely on *–ed* for this information. What we have done in (2) is structure the input so that *–ed* is no longer redundant and takes on a higher communicative value. Learners can no longer rely on content words or lexical items to get tense from the sentence.

What should be evident here is that redundancy is not absolute. Whether we can qualify a form as being redundant or not depends on the presence of other items in the input. Forms that are not redundant have higher communicative values and the higher the communicative value of a form, the more likely learners will pay attention to it and make form-meaning connections from it (P1c and P1d). When a form does not have any semantic value, it has no communicative value regardless of the presence or absence of redundancy. According to VanPatten, forms of low or no communicative value tend to be processed much later or perhaps not at all.

Subprinciple P1e states that learners can only process forms of lower communicative value if they have not exhausted their attentional resources from processing the input for meaning. In other words, if comprehension is difficult, they will not have enough attentional resources left over to allow them to pay attention to form. However, if the message is comprehensible, there is a greater chance (though still no guarantee) that they will also be able to attend to form.

Subprinciple P1f deals with how the position of a form may affect the likelihood of it getting processed. Consider the following sentences:

3) The Internet says that you can find great authentic Italian food in New York.

4) In New York, you can find great authentic Italian food.

Suppose the target form is the preposition *in*. In which sentence is the target form most salient? The answer is obviously (4). In (4), *in* is in initial position, which makes it more salient. Research (e.g., Barcroft & VanPatten, 1997; Rosa & O'Neill, 1998) has shown that forms that are in initial position are easiest to notice followed by forms in final position. Forms that are in medial position tend to be the most difficult to notice and process.

Principle 2

The second principle is also known as the first noun principle. This principle deals with how word order can affect how learners process input. A common word order in some languages such as English is subject-verb-object (SVO). However, some languages such as Spanish, do not always follow an SVO word order. In the following sentence, the first noun-phrase the learner encounters is not a subject but learners may very well attempt to encode it as such if they are used to an SVO order.

5) La vio Juan la fiesta anoche. (OVS)
her (object)　　saw Juan (subject)　　at the party last night
Juan saw her at the party last night.

Research has documented that when learners are confronted with such sentences, they have a tendency to encode pronouns and noun phrases as subjects. When this happens, they deliver incorrect intake data to the developing linguistic system. In this case, it is not that meaning is derived from a lexical item of another form; meaning is not gotten at all, or is gotten wrong.

The subprinciples of P2 illustrate that while learners have a tendency to rely on word order to process input, they may rely on other cues as well. These cues include lexical semantics (P2a), event probabilities (P2b), and context (P2c). Consider the following example in French:

6) Sophie fait acheter du lait à Julie.
    (lit. Sophie makes to buy some milk to Julie)
    Sophie has Julie buy some milk.

When confronted with such a sentence, learners of French have a tendency to (incorrectly) think that Sophie is the one who is buying the milk because Sophie is the first noun in the sentence (see VanPatten & Wong, 2004). Now examine the following example:

7) Le professeur fait faire les devoirs aux étudiants.
    (lit. The professor makes to do the homework to the students)
    The professor makes the students do the homework.

In this example, when asked who does homework, learners of French will likely say the students. However, it is important to point out that learners' correct response in this case does not necessarily mean that they have processed the sentence structure correctly to arrive at this correct answer. Unlike the first example where either Sophie or Julie could have logically performed the action (i.e., buy milk), there are lexical and contextual cues in this second example that limit the action of *doing homework* to the students. In the context of professor and students, it is typically professors who make students do homework and not the other way around. Thus, based on event probabilities and background knowledge about professors and students, learners might be able to interpret the sentence correctly. According to the subprinciples of Principle 2, when such cues are available, learners may abandon the first noun principle and rely on these cues instead.

To summarize, VanPatten's model of input processing is a theoretical model that describes how learners initially process input or how they make form-meaning connections from input. The principles and subprinciples of the model explain which features of input learners tend to pay attention to, which features they tend to ignore, and why. Based on this information, PI attempts to help learners abandon their inefficient processing strategies for more optimal ones so that better form-meaning connections are made.

The Components of PI

As described in its original conceptualization in VanPatten and Cadierno (1993), PI has three basic components:

- Learners are given information about how the target form or structure works, focusing on one form at a time.
- Learners are informed about a particular input processing strategy that might lead them to not notice and/or process the input incorrectly.
- Learners are given structured input (SI) activities—activities in which the input has been manipulated to push learners to rely on the target form in order to get meaning and/or to privilege the target structure in the input so that learners have a better chance of attending to it (Lee & VanPatten, 2003).

In this chapter, I will focus on the component of SI activities as an input enhancement technique because, as we will see in the discussion of PI research, SI activities are an effective means of getting learners to attend to and process form.

SI Activities as Input Enhancement

The activities used in PI are called **structured input** (SI) activities because the input has been manipulated or *structured* so that learners must rely on or attend to the target structure to interpret meaning. Thus, as an input enhancement technique, SI activities make target forms more salient. The nature of the activities themselves requires that learners attend to the target form and process it, that is to say, make correct form-meaning connections from it. This becomes clear when we examine how SI activities are created.

Creating SI Activities: Principle 1

Because SI activities are informed by the strategies that learners use to process input, the first step in creating an SI activity is to identify the processing strategy that learners are using to attempt to process the target form. Then, and only then, can we structure input so that learners abandon their inefficient strategies for more optimal ones. For example, suppose the target form in question is the simple past tense, the *passato prossimo*, in Italian. According to VanPatten's model of input processing, why might learners of Italian have difficulty noticing and processing past tense verb forms in the input? The answer is, evidently, Principle 1. As we saw earlier, the meaning of pastness can be encoded by temporal adverbs (content words) and by verbal morphology. According to Principle 1, if a content word and a grammatical form both encode the same semantic information, learners will rely on the content word first to get that information. Therefore, if we want to create SI activities to help learners process the *passato prossimo*, we need to structure the input in such a way that learners must rely exclusively on the verb forms to get the meaning of pastness. Let's look at an example of an SI activity for this form.

Activity 1a (Aural Rerential). *ieri o oggi*? You will hear sentences describing some things that Pietro did yesterday and some things that he is doing today. Listen carefully to the sentences and identify whether the sentence you hear is referring to something Pietro did yesterday (ieri) or is doing today (oggi) and determine whether Pietro was a good boy or bad boy yesterday. Circle the correct response.

1) Ieri   Oggi   3) Ieri   Oggi   5) Ieri   Oggi   7) Ieri   Oggi
2) Ieri   Oggi   4) Ieri   Oggi   6) Ieri   Oggi   8) Ieri   Oggi

Teacher's Script: Read the sentences once. Ask for an answer after each sentence. After reading all the sentences, ask the students if Pietro was a good boy yesterday or not.

1) Pulisce la casa (cleans house).
2) Ha data un cioccolatino al cane (gave chocolate to the dog).
3) Ha copiato il compito di matematica (copied the math homework).
4) Lavora per cinque ore (works for five hours).
5) Compra una pizza per i suoi amici (buys a pizza for his friends).
6) Ha ditto una bugia (told a lie).
7) Legge un libro (reads a book).
8) Ha dipino il gatto (painted the cat).

Follow-up: Do you think Pietro was a good boy or a bad boy yesterday? Raise your hand if you think Pietro was a good boy. Raise your hand if you think Pietro was a bad boy.

As you can see, the input in this SI activity was structured so that learners must attend to and process the verb forms correctly in order to determine the temporal reference of each sentence. Because learners tend to rely on content words such as *oggi* or *ieri* to get tense, these temporal adverbs were purposely not made available to learners so that they had to rely on verb forms alone to get this information. In other words, this activity was designed in such a way that learners must notice and process the form in order to do the exercise successfully. The following is an example of another referential activity in the written mode.

Activity 1b (Written Referential). The following are statements about your Italian instructor's activities. Determine if each activity mentioned happened last week (*la settimana passata*) or if it is an activity your instructor is doing today (*oggi*). Circle the correct response.

Lavora a l'ufficio (works at the office)	La settimana passata	Oggi
Ha guardato un film (watched a movie)	La settimana passata	Oggi
Mangia a casa (eats at home)	La settimana passata	Oggi
Prende un caffè (has a coffee)	La settimana passata	Oggi
Ha comprato una machina (bought a car)	La settimana passata	Oggi
Ha scritto un libro (wrote a book)	La settimana passata	Oggi

If you could choose, would you rather do the activities your instructor did last week or the activities she/he is doing today?

Once again, the sentences in Activity 1b were structured so that learners had to rely soley on the verb forms in order to determine temporal reference. Additionally, the verbs were purposely placed in initial position, the most salient position (P1f), to encourage noticing and processing of these forms.

Types of SI Activities

There are two types of SI activities: referential activities and affective activities. Activities 1a and 1b are referential activities. **Referential activities** require learners to pay attention to form in order to get meaning and have right or wrong answers so instructors can immediately verify if learners are making the correct form-meaning connections. **Affective activities**, on the other hand, do not necessarily have a right or wrong answer. Instead, they require learners to express an opinion, belief, or some other affective response. These activities give learners positive evidence containing the target form as they are engaged in processing information about the real world. The following is an example of an affective activity for the *passato prossimo*.

Activity 1c (Written Affective). Instant Messenger. You are on Instant Messenger with your mother and she asks you the usual questions to find out what you did yesterday. Below is a list of her customary questions. Simply write her an IM back for each question responding with yes (sì) or no based on what you actually did yesterday.

la vostro madre: Hai fatto colazione (Did you have breakfast)?
voi: _____
la vostro madre: Hai bevuto un cappuccino (Did you drink a capuccino)?
voi: _____
la vostro madre: Hai letto il giornale (Did you read the paper)?
voi: _____
la vostro madre: Hai mangiato da McDonald's (Did you eat at McDonald's)?
voi: _____
la vostro madre: Hai guardato la TV (Did you watch TV)?
voi: _____

Compare your answers with a classmate. Whose mother would be prouder?

Again, notice that the input has been structured so that the target forms are in the salient initial position.

Affective activities work very well in communicative classrooms because they encourage learners to give and receive meaningful and purposeful information. However, since it is the referential activities that allow instructors to determine whether learners have made correct form-meaning connections, it is recommended that instructors begin with these. The purpose of affective activities is to strengthen connections by providing learners with additional opportunities to see or hear target forms used in a meaningful context, as well as to encourage learners to respond to the content of the input.

Creating SI Activities: Principle 2

An example of a structure that deals with Principle 2, the First-Noun Principle, is the causative in French. The verb faire in French means "to do" or "to make" as in the following examples:
1) *Paul fait ses devoirs après le dîner.*
Paul does his homework after dinner.
2) *Ma mère fait un gâteau pour mon anniversaire chaque année.*
My mother makes a cake for my birthday every year.

The verb *faire* is also used to construct the causative structure. The French causative generally takes the form seen in the following examples:
3) Wynne fait promener le chien à Bill.
(lit. Wynne makes to walk the dog to Bill)
Wynne makes Bill walk the dog.
4) Anne fait faire un gâteau à Catherine.
(lit. Anne makes to make a cake to Catherine)
Anne makes Catherine make a cake.

In (3), there are two verbs and two subjects/agents. The first verb is *fait,* with its obligatorily preposed subject/agent *Wynne*. The second verb is *promener,* with its subject/agent, *Bill*, obligatorily placed post-verbally and marked by the preposition *à*. When L2 French learners are asked "Who walks the dog?" they have a tendency to (incorrectly) say "Wynne" because Wynne is the first noun that appears before the verb. Likewise in (4), when asked "Who makes the cake?" learners will (incorrectly) say "Anne" because Anne is the first subject in the sentence. This demonstrates learners' reliance on the First-Noun Principle (see VanPatten & Wong, 2004, as well as pretest data in Allen, 2000). When asked to give a rough translation of (3) and (4), learners typically say something like "Wynne walks the dog for Bill" or "Anne makes the cake for Catherine."

If we want to create SI activities to push learners away from this inefficient strategy, we would need to structure the input so that learners must rely on sentence structure in order to determine who is doing the action. An example of a referential activity for the causative structure is Activity 2a.

Activity 2a. (Aural Referential). Listen to each sentence, then indicate who is performing the action by answering each question.
1) Who cleans the room?
2) Who packs the bags?
3) Who watches the movie?
4) Who plays the flute?
5) Who does the dishes?
6) Who buys wine?
7) Who cooks dinner?
8) Who washes the car?

Teacher's Script:
1) *Claude fait nettoyer la chambre à Richard* (Claude makes Richard clean the room).
2) *Marc fait les valises pour Jean* (Marc packs the bags for Jean).
3) *Sandra fait voir le film à Pierre* (Sandra makes Pierre see the movie).
4) *Thierry fait jouer de la flute à Paul* (Thierry makes Paul play the flute).
5) *Louis fait la vaisselle au lieu de Vincent* (Louis does the dishes instead of Vincent).
6) *Caroline fait acheter du vin à Marie* (Caroline makes Marie buy some wine).
7) *Candice fait la cuisine pour Pauline* (Candice cooks dinner for Pauline).
8) *Pierre fait laver la voiture à Dennis* (Pierre makes Dennis wash the car).

In Activity 2a, learners must listen to a series of sentences containing the verb *faire* and determine who is performing each activity. Notice that we do not merely give students sentences containing the target structure, that is to say, the causative. If we only provided learners with sentences containing the causative construction "*X fait Y à Z*," there is a chance that students may respond correctly based on pattern memorization and not because they have made any kind of form-meaning connection. In order to gage whether learners are indeed processing sentence structure for meaning (i.e., to determine who is doing the action), we have to include the noncausative with the verb *faire* along with causative *faire* constructions. Therefore, noncausative sentences, such as *Candice fait la cuisine pour Pauline* (Candice cooks dinner for Pauline), were also included. In this way, learners are required to rely on sentence structure to determine who is doing each activity. Notice also that the input in this activity was manipulated so that learners cannot use lexical semantics (P2a), event probabilities (P2b), or context (P2c) to help them interpret the sentences. In Activity 2a, either one of the two people in each sentence could logically be the one doing the action. Because the goal of the SI activity is to force learners to rely exclusively on sentence structure for meaning, we must remove elements from the activities that allow learners to give correct responses without noticing or relying on sentence structure. To recap, input was structured in Activity 2a by (1) including both causative and noncausative sentences so learners cannot rely on pattern memorization to interpret meaning and (2) by making sure that sentences do not allow learners to rely on event probabilities or background knowledge. Activity 2b is an example of an affective activity for the causative construction to provide further opportunities for learners to connect meaning to form as well as to express themselves communicatively (see VanPatten & Wong, 2004 and Lee & VanPatten, 2003, for additional examples of SI activities for the French causative).

Activity 2b (Written Affective). Read each sentence. Then decide whether or not it is typical of a parent-child relationship. Imagine that the child is 10 years old.

Un parent…(A parent)

1) *fait faire les devoirs à son enfant.* *C'est typique /Ce n'est pas typique*
(makes his/her child do homework)
2) *fait étudier la musique à son enfant.* *C'est typique /Ce n'est pas typique*
(makes his/her child study music)
3) *fait faire du jogging à son enfant.* *C'est typique /Ce n'est pas typique*
(makes his/her child go jogging)
4) *fait nettoyer la salle de bain à son enfant.* *C'est typique /Ce n'est pas typique*
(makes his/her child clean the bathroom)
5) *fait promener le chien à son enfant.* *C'est typique /Ce n'est pas typique*
(makes his/her child walk the dog)
6) *fait lire le journal à son enfant.* *C'est typique /Ce n'est pas typique*
(makes his/her child read the newspaper)
7) *fait se laver les mains à son enfant.* *C'est typique /Ce n'est pas typique*
(makes his/her child wash his/her hands)

Now, repeat the above but this time imagine that the child is 18 and still at home. Do any answers change?

Activity 2b Teacher's Note. When reviewing the activity as a group, you read the item out loud and students respond with *C'est typique* or *Ce n'est pas typique*. Students do not repeat or otherwise produce the structure.

Guidelines

As pointed out earlier in this chapter, the most critical step in designing SI activities is to first determine why learners are having difficulty processing the particular target form or structure. What strategies are learners using that are causing them to ignore and/or process the form inefficiently or incorrectly? Is it due to a reliance on lexical items (P1)? Is it due to a word order problem (P2)? Does the location of the form make it difficult to notice and process (P1f)? Or is it some combination of these factors? Keep in mind that the primary goal of SI activities is to help learners abandon inefficient processing strategies for more optimal ones. Therefore, if the processing problem or strategy is not identified, we would not be able to create SI activities to help them reach this goal. Lee and VanPatten (1995, 2003) provide a set of guidelines to help instructors create and implement SI activities in the classroom. The following were adapted from Lee and VanPatten (2003) and Wong (2005):

1) Present one thing at a time. This means that only one rule of usage and/or one form of a paradigm should be presented at a time. When learners can focus on one form at a time, they will be more likely to pay attention.

2) Keep meaning in focus. In order for form-meaning connections to occur, learners must attend to both meaning and form. If an activity can be completed without attention to meaning, then it is not an SI activity.

3) Move from sentences to connected discourse. It is preferable to begin with sentences first because short sentences are easier to process than connected discourse. When comprehension does not require a lot of effort, there is a greater chance that learners will pay attention to the relevant grammatical information that is the target of instruction.

4) Use both aural and written input. Both aural and written input should be used in SI activities because learners should have opportunities to receive input in both modalities. While all learners need aural input, more visual learners would benefit from "seeing" the input as well.

5) Have learners do something with the input. This guideline goes hand in hand with the goals of communicative language teaching. The activities should not only be meaningful, they should also be purposeful. This means that learners must have a reason for attending to the input. Therefore, activities should have learners respond to the input in some way to ensure that they are actively engaged in its processing.

6) Keep the learners' processing strategies in mind. We have already discussed the importance of this point and it cannot be stressed enough. This guideline is in fact what distinguishes SI activities from other input enhancement techniques. Because the goal of SI activities is to help learners move away from inefficient processing strategies so that they adopt more optimal ones, these strategies must be kept in mind while creating activities (see Wong, 2004a for a detailed discussion).

Evidence from Research

There is a substantial amount of empirical data to support the effectiveness of PI and SI activities as an input enhancement technique in a variety of L2s. Empirical studies that have compared PI (operationalized as explicit information followed by referential and affective SI activities) to traditional instruction (TI) (operationalized as explicit information followed by mechanical, meaningful, and communicative drills) overwhelmingly show that PI is better than TI on sentence level interpretation tasks and that PI is as good or better than TI on sentence level production tasks. These studies include Benati (2001) (Italian future tense), Cadierno (1995) (Spanish preterite tense), Cheng (2004) (Spanish *ser* vs *estar*), VanPatten and Cadierno (1993) (Spanish object pronouns), and VanPatten and Wong (2004) (French causative). VanPatten and Sanz (1995) demonstrated that the effects of PI can also be generalized to assessment measures that involve more complex cognitive processing such as a video narration task. In another series of studies, there is data to support the notion that the positive results of PI are due to SI activities and not to the explicit information that is a component of PI. These studies include Benati (2004), Sanz and Morgan-Short (2004), VanPatten and Oikennon (1996), and Wong (2004b). A longitudinal study by VanPatten and Fernandez (2004) has data to show that the effects of PI are durable for up to eight months. For detailed discussions of these studies, please consult the volume edited by VanPatten (2004).

SI Activities and Other Input Enhancement

As discussed in the previous section, SI activities have been and continue to be the subject of much research with favorable results. However, research on other types of input enhancement, such as input flood and textual enhancement, has produced less consistent findings (see Wong, 2005). What makes SI activities stand out from other input enhancement techniques that also attempt to make target forms more salient? The answer is the following: SI activities as input enhancement *go beyond* making forms more salient. The activities (when done correctly) are set up so that learners must notice and process target forms correctly. SI activities are directly informed by the strategies that learners use to process input. In other words, these activities are created based on an understanding of why learners may have difficulty noticing and processing a particular target form. Additionally, SI activities are designed so that learners have no choice but to rely exclusively on the target form or structure for meaning. While some other input enhancement techniques may make target forms more salient, instructors cannot always assess whether learners are indeed noticing and processing the forms. The very nature of SI activities, on the other hand, necessitates that target forms are noticed and processed correctly.

Questions and Topics for Discussion

1) An example of a form that does not have inherent semantic value is the third person singular –*s* as in *she speaks*. The –*s* does not have inherent semantic value because it does not express any meaning. Can you think of (other) examples of forms that do not have inherent semantic value in the language that you teach?
2) What is the difference between input processing and processing instruction?
3) What are some examples of processing problems in the language that you teach that can be explained by the model of input processing? How might you design SI activities to help learners notice and process these target forms?
4) What is the difference between referential and affective SI activities? Why might it be important to include both in the classroom?
5) How are SI activities different from other types of input or comprehension-based classroom activities?
6) What makes SI activities unique as a form of input enhancement?

Notes

I would like to thank Adela Lechintan and Frank Sbrocchi for their assistance in creating the Italian sample activities.

References

Allen, L.Q. (2000). Form-meaning connections and the French causative: An experiment in processing instruction. *Studies in Second Language Acquisition, 22*, 69-84.

Barcroft, J., & VanPatten, B. (1997). Acoustic salience: Testing location, stress and the boundedness of grammatical form in second language acquisition input processing. In A.T. Pérez-Leroux & W.R. Glass (Eds.), *Contemporary perspectives on the acquisition of Spanish: Vol. 2. Production, processing, and comprehension* (pp. 109-121). Somerville, MA: Cascadilla Press.

Benati, A. (2001). A comparative study of the effects of processing instruction and output-based instruction on the acquisition of the Italian future tense. *Language Teaching Research, 5,* 95-127.

Benati, A. (2004). The effects of structured input activities and explicit information on the acquisition of Italian tense. In B. VanPatten (Ed.), *Processing instruction: Theory, research, and commentary* (pp. 207-225). Mahwah, NJ: Lawrence Erlbaum.

Cadierno, T. (1995). Formal instruction in processing perspective: An investigation into the Spanish past tense. *The Modern Language Journal, 79,* 179-194.

Cheng, A. (2004). Processing instruction and Spanish *ser* and *estar*: Forms with semantic-aspectual values. In B. VanPatten (Ed.), *Processing instruction: Theory, research, and commentary* (pp. 119-141). Mahwah, NJ: Lawrence Erlbaum.

Farley, A. (2004). Processing instruction and the Spanish subjunctive: Is explicit information needed? In B. VanPatten (Ed.), *Processing instruction: Theory, research, and commentary* (pp. 227-239). Mahwah, NJ: Lawrence Erlbaum.

Lee, J.F., Cadierno, T., Glass, W.R., & VanPatten, B. (1997). The effects of lexical and grammatical cues on processing tense in second language input. *Applied Language Learning, 8,* 1-23.

Lee, J.F., & VanPatten, B. (1995). *Making communicative language teaching happen.* New York: McGraw-Hill.

Lee, J.F., & VanPatten, B. (2003). *Making communicative language teaching happen,* 2nd edition. New York: McGraw-Hill.

Musumeci, D. (1989). *The ability of second language learners to assign tense at the sentence level.* Unpublished doctoral dissertation, University of Illinois, Urbana-Champaign.

Rosa, E., & O'Neill, M. (1998). Effects of stress and location on acoustic salience at the initial stages of Spanish L2 input processing. *Spanish Applied Linguistics, 2,* 24-52.

Sanz, C., & Morgan-Short, K. (2004). Positive evidence versus explicit rule presentation and explicit negative feedback: A computer-assisted study. *Language Learning, 54,* 35-78.

VanPatten, B. (1993). Grammar teaching for the acquisition-rich classroom. *Foreign Language Annals, 26,* 435-450.

VanPatten, B. (1996). *Input processing and grammar instruction.* Norwood, NJ: Ablex.

VanPatten, B. (2002). Communicative classrooms, processing instruction, and pedagogical norms. In S. Gass, K. Bardovi-Harli, S. Sieloff Magnon, & J. Walz (Eds.), *Pedagogical norms for second and foreign language learning and teaching: Studies in honor of Albert Valdman* (pp. 105-118). Amsterdam: John Benjamins.

VanPatten, B. (2004). *Processing instruction: Theory, research, and commentary*. Mahwah, NJ: Lawrence Erlbaum.

VanPatten, B. & Cadierno, T. (1993). Explicit instruction and input processing. *Studies in Second Language Acquisition, 15,* 225-243.

VanPatten, B., & Fernandez, C. (2004). The long-term effects of processing instruction. In B. VanPatten (Ed.), *Processing instruction: Theory, research, and commentary* (pp. 273-289). Mahwah, NJ: Lawrence Erlbaum.

VanPatten, B., & Oikennon, S. (1996). Explanation versus structured input in processing instruction. *Studies in Second Language Acquisition, 18,* 495-510.

VanPatten, B., & Sanz, C. (1995). From input to output: Processing instruction and communicative tasks. In F. Eckman, D. Highland, P. Lee, J. Mileham & R. Rutkowski Weber (Eds.), *Second language acquisition theory and pedagogy* (pp. 169-185). Mahwah, NJ: Lawrence Erlbaum.

VanPatten, B., & Wong, W. (2004). Processing instruction and the French causative: A replication. In B. VanPatten (Ed.), *Processing instruction: Theory, research, and commentary* (pp. 97-118). Mahwah, NJ: Lawrence Erlbaum.

Wong, W. (2002). Linking form and meaning: Processing instruction. *The French Review, 76,* 236-264.

Wong, W. (2004a). The nature of processing instruction. In B. VanPatten (Ed.), *Processing instruction: Theory, research, and commentary* (pp. 33-63). Mahwah, NJ: Lawrence Erlbaum.

Wong, W. (2004b). Processing instruction in French: The roles of explicit information and structured input. In B. VanPatten (Ed.), *Processing instruction: Theory, research, and commentary* (pp. 187-205). Mahwah, NJ: Lawrence Erlbaum.

Wong, W. (2005). *Input enhancement: From theory and research to the classroom*. New York: McGraw-Hill.

Chapter 7
The Role of Interaction in Input Enhancement

Jessica Williams, University of Illinois at Chicago
Claudia Fernandez, DePaul University

Input enhancement is a term that has been used in a variety of ways, both in this volume and in other contexts. It is therefore worthwhile to clarify the definition of both words in the term. **Input**, simply put, is language that the learner reads or hears, provided that it carries some communicative intention. Input would therefore exclude utterances simply *about* language, such as *Spanish has two words for be* or *the comparative in English is formed by adding -er to the end of an adjective or adverb.* **Input enhancement**, as we are defining it, is any change in input that is intended to or has the effect of making some aspect of the input more available for further processing.

It is important to note that since the term was first introduced by Sharwood Smith in 1981, it has been used in a variety of ways, often with somewhat different implications. Sharwood Smith presented it as any conscious pedagogical decision by a teacher or materials writer to draw learners' attention to input in order to facilitate the learning process. This includes a range of techniques from the provision of metalinguistic information to emphatic hand gestures. Doughty and Williams (1998) took a more constrained view, limiting their discussion of input enhancement to textual (e.g., White, 1998; Wong, 2003) and intonational enhancement (e.g., Doughty & Varela, 1998).

Wong's (2005) volume on input enhancement includes textual enhancement but also input floods, structured input activities, and consciousness raising tasks. This view, like Sharwood Smith's, is broader, but like earlier definitions, is essentially a pedagogical one. These are all techniques that a teacher might employ to draw learners' attention to important aspects of the input.

This chapter will focus on still another vehicle through which learners' attention may be directed at input: through interaction. This differs in two important and related ways from earlier definitions. First, as the term implies, the enhancement of input results from the learner's interaction with an interlocutor. We are therefore limiting our discussion to spoken language (It is in principle possible to consider teacher feedback on written work as a form of interaction; see, for example, Ayoun, 2001, 2004). Second, and as a result of the first difference, it is difficult for teachers to plan interaction that will enhance a preselected target form (Foster, 1998) because interactional enhancement of input rests more in the hands of learners and their interlocutors. Teachers can design activities that foster interaction, and they can provide feedback within interaction, but they cannot predict the aspects of language on which learners will focus during that interaction.

Triggers for Interactional Enhancement

We will consider three main forms of interactional enhancement: feedback, negotiation, and requests for or offers of assistance. Before considering each in detail, however, it is important to establish the context in which these sequences occur and what triggers them. All three occur as part of **language related episodes** (LREs), which are interactional sequences where learners focus on their use of language, or are encouraged to do so by others (Leesser, 2004; Swain, 1995; Williams, 1999). A broader term, **focus on form episodes**, (FFEs) has also been used, primarily by Ellis and his colleagues (e.g., Ellis, Basturkmen, & Loewen, 2001a, 2001b; Loewen, 2003, 2004, 2005). LREs all begin with a learner **trigger,** whereas FFEs may also be initiated by the teacher.

The central feature of triggers in LREs and FFEs is a perceived or actual problem in communication; it is this interactional turn that initiates or *triggers* the episode. Problems may come in several forms. The problem may be in comprehension as in Example 1. Here, the trigger is the word *nutrition* in line 4, and the first student (S_1) signals non-comprehension in line 5. The interlocutor (S_2) modifies the output (which is, of course, learner input) to accommodate S_1's needs. S_2 then provides a definition of the word *nutrition* in line 6.

Example 1 (S=student)[1]
1) S_1: (reading) The infant mortality rate in America has fallen dramatically.
2) S_2: Yeah.
3) S_1: How do you think? What is the reason?
4) S_2: Maybe I think the nutrition or—
5) S_1: trish?
6) S_2: Nutrition for the mother and for baby. Something like they eat better food and vitamins.

Second, the problem may be in learner output: learner production may fall short of the target, perhaps hampering communication, as in Example 2, or perhaps eliciting a corrective or clarifying response from the interlocutor. In this example, it seems that the trigger is a combination of nontarget-like pronunciation (*one* instead of *want*) and the lack of *to* in the infinitive that leads to a brief communication breakdown. Negotiation continues for several turns and ends with the speaker (S_1) modifying her utterance in the direction of the target in line 5.

Example 2 (S=student)
1) S_1: The president had a speech about ten minutes. So I have some question about his speech. What part of budget he didn't [wan] cut? What part of budget he [wan] cut?
2) S_2: One cut? Two cut?
3) S_3: What? He cut.
4) S_2: One cut.
5) S_1: One major. What part of budget the president didn't **want to** cut? He don't **want to** cut the budget.

A third possibility also stems from output problems, what might be called **learner need**. If learners are having difficulty expressing their communicative intention or wish for greater accuracy and effectiveness in their production, they may appeal for assistance, as in Example 3.

Example 3 (S=student)
1) S_1: I have a question. What do we call when we speaking like this (whispers)? What's the verb about that?
2) S_2: Whisper. Whisper.

3) S₁: Whisper?
4) S₂: Yeah.
5) S₁: Whisper.
6) S₂: Yeah, whisper.
7) S₁: Silent murmer. Murmer maybe.
8) S₂: Murmer is about religious a little bit.
9) S₁: Really murmer?
10) S₂: The other is whisper W-H-I-
11) S₁: H? no.
12) S₂: W-H-I-S-P-E-R.
13) S₁: Whisper.

Such appeals are not always direct. For example, an interlocutor may interpret hesitation as an implicit appeal for assistance and offer a suggestion or finish an utterance for the other speaker (Foster & Ohta, 2005).

The final episode includes *potential* problems, as perceived by the teacher or interlocutor, as a trigger for input enhancement. Ellis, et al. (2001b) refer to this as a **preemptive focus on form**. Thus, even if learners have not experienced difficulty with the input, an interlocutor (usually a teacher) may anticipate potential problems and enhance input as part of the interaction, as in Example 4 where the teacher anticipates learner difficulty with an unfamiliar lexical item, *finite*.

Example 4 (T=teacher, S=student)
1) S: (reading) A group of related words with a subject and a finite verb.
2) T: Mmhm. S (student's name), what's a clause?
3) S: A group of related words with a subject and a finite verb.
4) T: Right, now. What do I mean by finite? Does anyone know what this word means? It's a fancy word. We use it in mathematics sometimes. It means the opposite of infinite. Something that has an end. A definite end. So if I have this line—it has a beginning and it has an end. This is finite. It has a beginning and an end.

In summary, triggers for interactional enhancement of input include problems in comprehension, non-targetlike output, actual learner need, and other perceived learner needs.

Types of Interactional Enhancement of Input

To some extent, the type of situation that triggers input enhancement will specify the type of LRE/FFE in which the enhancement takes place. A breakdown in communication will most likely initiate some form of negotiation, especially in convergent classroom activities, such as information gap tasks. If meaning is unclear, interlocutors generally try to negotiate until meaning is clarified and communication is reestablished (de la Fuente, 2002; Ellis, 1999; Mackey, 1999; Oliver, 1995; Pica, 2002; Shehadeh, 1999, 2001). For example, the interlocutor may rephrase or change the form of the original input. This type of adjustment serves to extend or elaborate the **positive evidence** that the learner receives; that is, it provides the learner with information about what is possible in the target language.

In Example 5, the learner attempts to pronounce what appears to be an unfamiliar term. The teacher repeats the word in context, provides a gloss, and then repeats it slowly with stress. The learner acknowledges his understanding with a comment.

Example 5 (T=teacher, S=student)
1) T: What about the guy with the yellow vest and the woman with the blue dress?
2) S_1: Just—new neighbor?
3) T: New neighbors. Perhaps. Maybe a new couple.
4) S_2: [kaep—]?
5) T: A new couple.
6) S_2: [kuhpr]?
7) T: They just had a wedding. **[Kuh..pl]**
8) S_2: I think they just get married.

Negotiation sequences are not strictly limited to instances of communicative breakdown. They may also occur over linguistic form when communication is not at risk, as part of speakers' desire to express their intentions accurately or to assist one another (Ellis et al., 2001a; Foster & Ohta, 2005; Ohta, 2000; Pica, 2002). If the problem is due to learner output that is nontarget-like, but does not impede communication, then some type of corrective or clarifying feedback is more likely, especially in classroom settings. Feedback may be given in a single turn, or as part of a more lengthy negotiation. It may be explicit or implicit, and it may provide positive evidence, negative evidence, or both. Finally, it may or may not require or even allow a learner response (Lyster, 1998a, 2004; Lyster & Ranta, 1997; Oliver, 1995). Example 6 contains both positive and **negative evidence**, that is, information about what is not possible in the target language.

Example 6 (T=teacher, S=student)
1) T: Any examples of skills or talents?
2) S: I'm pretty good typing.
3) T: You're pretty good at typing. Notice at. Notice how you use at. I'm very good at typing.
4) S: Why at? at? Why at and not in?
5) T: It has to do with the meaning of the word. It's the word you use.
6) S: I can't say, "I'm good typing?" I can't say that?
7) T: You can't say what?
8) S: I'm good typing?
9) T: No.
10) S: No? I need to put the at -the preposition before?
11) T: Right.
12) S: Good...at...typing. (Slowly as she writes).

Negative evidence is seen as an indirect form of input enhancement in that it may prime the learner to scan future input for relevant information. It does not affect input in the immediate situation because, according to our definition, it provides no input. Only positive evidence can be regarded as input. From the perspective of input enhancement, the positive evidence contained in certain types of feedback, such as **recasts,** is most relevant to our discussion. In a recast, the non-targetlike utterance of a learner is reformulated as a targetlike utterance with the original meaning essentially preserved. In recasts, as well as explicit corrections, learners hear a targetlike version of their original utterance. In addition, both recasts and explicit corrections can provide negative evidence, or an indication to learners that they have done something wrong. However, in a recast the interlocutor or teacher may not clearly indicate that an error has been made, and thus the learner may not perceive the negative evidence it contains.

Prompts are another common type of error feedback. They

are responses that push learners to reconsider their production and retrieve target forms they already know, but perhaps do not fully control. Prompts include moves such as elicitation, clarification requests, clues, and repetition of the learner utterance with problematic aspects highlighted in some way (Lyster, 2004; Panova & Lyster, 2002). An important feature of prompts is that they do not include the target utterance and therefore, with the possible exception of clues, must be considered a form of negative evidence, not input.

Finally, triggers that involve learner need, whether articulated by the learner or anticipated by the teacher or interlocutor, are likely to yield episodes that involve requests for, or offers of, assistance. In Example 7, students are looking at a text in pairs. S_1 anticipates that S_2 will have difficulty with the term *hitchhike*.

Example 7 (S=student)
1) S_1: Hitchhiking, you know?
2) S_2: No.
3) S_1: Like you don't have car but you want to move another city and you (puts out thumb).
4) S_2: Oh, OK hitch hike. How do you spe—no, how do you pronounce it?
5) S_1: **Hitch...hike**.
6) S_2: Hitchhike. OK.

Impact of Input Enhancement

The impact of input enhancement can be considered in two phases. First, there is the possibility that the input itself has been changed in a way that makes it easier to process. Second, we must consider the impact of the enhanced input on interlanguage processes. In what way does the enhanced input foster learning processes? We begin with the first.

Direct Impact on Input

Second language acquisition research has explored two primary effects of input enhancement: (1) increased **salience** and (2) increased **comprehensibility**. The salience of novel input during interaction can be increased in several ways. Probably the most obvious is to emphasize the input or specific aspects of the input. In spoken interaction, this would be done acoustically; that is, target input would be uttered with higher pitch or increased volume, enhancing the positive evidence.

It is also possible to enhance negative evidence by highlighting the gap between nontarget-like learner production and a target-like recast (Doughty & Varela, 1998; Muranoi, 2000; Nobuyoshi & Ellis, 1993). Example 8 contains both. In line 2, the teacher repeats the nontarget-like utterance, providing potential negative evidence. In line 4, she provides a recast, essentially, positive evidence. In both cases, she adds emphasis to the relevant aspects of the evidence.

Example 8
    1) José: I think that the worm will go under the soil.
    2) Teacher: I **think** that the worm **will** go under the soil?
    3) José: (no response)
    4) Teacher: I **thought** that the worm **would** go under the soil.
    5) José: I **thought** that the worm **would** go under the soil.
(Doughty & Varela, 1998, p. 124, emphasis in original)

Input may also be enhanced through segmentation, a process in which input is broken down into shorter or smaller pieces, again perhaps making it easier to process. This can be seen in Example 5 where the teacher repeats the word *couple* slowly in separate stressed syllables. Finally, research in both psycholinguistics (e.g., Neisser, 1967) and second language acquisition (e.g., Barcroft & VanPatten, 1997; Klein, 1986) has suggested that the position of an item in an utterance can increase its salience, wherein the initial position is the most powerful. Therefore, a speaker can enhance the salience of a word or structure by fronting it. Example 9 contains elements of both segmentation and fronting. S_1 first works to ensure S_2's understanding of *St. John* and then of *murderer*.

Example 9 (S=student)
    1) S_1:   OK. Who is the murderer in St. John Antigua?
    2) S_2:   Who is?
    3) S_1:   Who is the murderer in St. John? You understand my question?
    4) S_2:   No...OK
    5) S_1:   St. John. Remember the Caribbean...Caribbean island? St. John.
    6) S_2:   St. John.
    7) S_1:   A murder in St. John. Killer. The murder. Who is it?
    8) S_2:   Killer. Criminal. Killed someone. I don't know.

Finally, input enhancement may involve the provision of metalinguistic information, as in Example 6, where the teacher draws the learner's attention to the preposition *at*. This kind of information does not fit our definition of input, and therefore cannot be considered a direct form of input enhancement. Yet, it may help learners notice these features in future input and therefore may be considered an indirect method of input enhancement. Basturkmen, Loewen, and Ellis (2001) suggest that this kind of information has an impact when the episode is initiated by the learner, as in a request for assistance.

The effects of increased salience cannot always be disentangled from the main objective of input enhancement: increased comprehensibility. Indeed, although the fronting and segmentation shown in Example 9 may increase saliency, the ultimate goal is to increase the comprehensibility of the message. Comprehensibility may also be increased by simplifying or elaborating input. In Example 10, in response to a learner question, the teacher provides a simplified explanation of an idiomatic expression, perhaps sacrificing some semantic detail.

Example 10 (S= student, T=teacher)
1) S: I heard the chicken head cut off. Why he cut the chicken head cut off?
2) T: Oh. Like a chicken with its head cut off. It's just an idiom. It means hurry, rush. He's rushing.

In contrast, in Example 11 she elaborates the meaning of *cart*:

Example 11 (T=teacher)
1) T: Not carriage. Cart. Yeah. OK. There's also carts that we used. Just a wooden box with wheels…For poor people. They couldn't buy a carriage.

Elaborative information can include pronunciation, spelling, definitions, synonyms, or other explicit information. Again, some of the more explicit information does not fit our definition of input and should be regarded as an effort to enhance future input.

Impact on Interlanguage Processes

A number of studies have attempted to measure the effect of enhancements on interlanguage processes. For example, the presumed desired effect of increased salience is a corresponding increase in **no-**

ticing. Noticing is considered by many (Gass, 1997; Robinson, 1995; Schmidt, 1995, 2001) to be a necessary step in the acquisition process. Increasing the salience of positive evidence may help learners notice features that they had previously ignored. The provision of negative evidence, on the other hand, may allow learners to engage in cognitive comparison, that is, to compare their own production, which they now realize falls short of the target, with incoming input, in a process that is often called **noticing the gap** (Schmidt & Frota, 1986).

A complementary perspective on the relationship between input enhancement and noticing relates to when the noticing occurs. When input enhancement includes the provision of new, modified input, in other words, positive evidence, then it is possible for learners to notice the enhanced input immediately, perhaps beginning the process of making form-meaning connections. If, however, input enhancement is considered more broadly, to include negative evidence and metalinguistic information, which, by definition, are not input, the horizon for noticing is extended considerably. Such information might affect interlanguage processes in two ways. First, if moves that provide this information lead to immediate modification of learner output in the direction of the target, this could create a sort of auto-input enhancement. More likely, however, is that the negative evidence will result in no immediate enhancement of input. Rather, it may have a priming effect. In other words, this information may alert learners to important aspects of future input that they had not noticed in the past.

Increased comprehensibility may also have two effects on processing; first is the obvious potential increase in comprehension, already discussed. It has been argued that learners cannot learn what they do not comprehend (Gass, 1997; Krashen, 1985) and therefore, that comprehension should be considered a necessary step toward acquisition. In addition, higher levels of comprehension may free up learner attention that can then be devoted to noticing more formal aspects of the input (VanPatten, 1990, 1996). These possibilities have been investigated in a variety of experimental and classroom settings, providing evidence that interaction aids comprehension. When comparing interactionally modified input with premodified or unmodified input, a number of studies found that learners comprehend better when they have the opportunity to negotiate than when they are only exposed to input, even if that input has already been modified to assist comprehension (e.g., de la Fuente, 2002; Ellis, Tanaka, & Yamazaki, 1994; Loschky, 1994; Pica, Doughty, & Young, 1986; Pica, Young, & Doughty, 1987). The advantage of interaction over input exposure alone is that it offers learners the possibility of targeting aspects of the input that they have not understood, and negotiating their meaning through clarification requests or comprehension checks. However, as necessary as comprehension is for acquisition, research has been mixed regarding the effects of comprehension-in-interaction on acquisition (e.g., Ellis et al., 1994; Loschky, 1994; Mackey, 1999). Within interaction, one form of learner response, **uptake**, has been defined as a response move that immediately follows feedback (Lyster & Ranta, 1997). Successful uptake demonstrates that the learner has understood or can use the form that has been the focus of the episode (Ellis et al., 2001a). In Example 12, the learner uses the non-target like *fabrik* in line 1. He acknowledges the feedback with a repetition in line 3, and with *yes* in line 5. Both are considered forms of successful uptake.

Example 12 (S=student, T=teacher)
    1) S: The machine do all for the man. I visit the chocolate fabrik and I know—
    2) T: —factory.
    3) S: Factory and they make the M.?
    4) T: M&Ms.
    5) S: Yes.

Still, it is not clear exactly what uptake means. Does a response such as the one in Example 12 mean that input has been processed? If so, has it been processed for acquisition or merely for momentary comprehension? Or is it simply a way of greasing the wheels of polite interaction? On this we can only speculate. However, incorporation of the feedback move into a modified learner utterance does suggest that the mismatch has been noticed, and if learners can attach meaning to the form in focus, the input then becomes **intake**. Intake is the result of input processing. For input to become intake, it not only needs to be noticed, but it also needs to be processed; that is, the learner must make the connection between the new form and its meaning. If the learner incorporates feedback into an utterance, this might be an indication that the new form has been both noticed and processed and that it is available for potential incorporation into the developing system.

On the other hand, if the learner does not respond with a form of uptake, does it mean that the feedback has not been noticed and therefore is not available for intake? It is clear from an increasing number of studies (e.g., de la Fuente, 2002; Mackey & Philp, 1998; Ohta, 2000) that uptake is not necessary for acquisition. That is, the fact that learners do not uptake the feedback does not necessarily mean that they have not noticed or processed the input. Yet, there is increasing evidence for the existence of a relationship between uptake and acquisition.

Loewen (2005) demonstrates a clear connection between uptake and subsequent accurate production, although as he notes, the reasons for this are not entirely clear. Since it seems unlikely that a single prompted production would result in immediate acquisition, it is important to consider carefully the implications of uptake. Does the act of production help them to notice the new form? Or might uptake merely reflect the consolidation of a form already well along in the acquisition process? At this point, we cannot be certain. What successful uptake does imply is that learners have noticed and understood the form in focus. The fact that the learner's utterance merited feedback in the first place indicates that either the form was (1) new for the learner or (2) already processed but still not under full control. If the form was new, and the learner responds with uptake, this suggests that he or she has noticed, but might not be ready to incorporate it into the developing system. Most likely, learners need more exposure to this new form as well as opportunities to access it for production. On the other hand, if the form has been previously processed but is not yet under full control, the feedback received during interaction and the subsequent incorporation of the form in the learner utterance suggest consolidation of a form that is already part of the developing system.

Factors in the Effectiveness of Input Enhancement

If we assume that interactionally enhanced input can facilitate interlanguage processes, we must then turn to the question of what aspects of the enhancement appear to be most effective?

- Does the length, complexity, or intensity of the interaction make a difference?
- Is it the positive or the negative evidence that provides the information language learners need in order to develop proficiency?
- Do the participants in the interaction make a difference?

For these questions we have some preliminary answers. Ellis et al. (2001b) demonstrate that more complex, negotiated interaction, in which learners have the opportunity to negotiate extensively around a communication problem, yields more successful uptake (within their definition—the incorporation of the correct linguistic form in subsequent production) than short opportunities for negotiation. This may be the case because extended negotiation is a sign of learner persistence. If learners pursue negotiation to its logical end, the result is comprehension. Once learners have comprehended, it is more likely that they will integrate such a form in subsequent production. Yet, longer is not always better, at least not in the case of feedback. Both Han (2002) and Philp (2003) report that for recasts, shorter, simpler turns are more likely to lead to successful subsequent production. Their results also suggest that narrowly but intensively targeted recasts are likely to be perceived as corrective feedback and perhaps for this reason, have significant impact. Ellis (2001) has referred to this as **intensive** treatment, in which a few target items are preselected for feedback, contrasting it with **extensive** treatment, where feedback is provided in a more ad hoc, but perhaps natural classroom manner.

There is some debate as to whether learners benefit more from the positive or negative evidence provided in negotiation and various forms of feedback, in particular recasts. A number of studies have demonstrated that recasts lead to successful uptake, and facilitate the acquisition of linguistic forms, as measured in oral and written immediate posttests (Ellis et al., 2001a; Han, 2002; Iwashita, 2003; Leeman, 2003; Loewen, 2005; Mackey & Philp, 1998; Philp, 2003). It seems that learners who do notice the mismatch between what they have said and what they should have said are likely to uptake the new information, and are able to recall the form in focus in immediate post-tests. Leeman (2003), comparing the negative and positive evidence contained in the recasts, concluded that it is the opportunities for learners to process the form when they listen to it, that is, the positive evidence in the recast, that is particularly beneficial. However, providing positive evidence in the absence of learner requests for it (i.e., preemptive positive evidence) seems to be less beneficial than when it is given as a result of a communicative need (Iwashita, 2003; Long, Inagaki, & Ortega, 1998).

The results of experimental studies point to the constructive impact of recasts, yet they seem less effective for learners in content-based L2 instruction. It has been reported that these learners do not perceive recasts as a sign of correction and interpret them as just another way of saying the same thing (Lyster, 1998a, 1998b, 2004; Lyster & Ranta, 1997; Pica, 2002). It is possible that the content focus of these classes reduces the effectiveness of recasts (Lyster, 2004; Sheen, 2004). Teachers and learners are focused on meaning during interaction since the main instructional goal is the learning of content. Teachers tend to repeat learners' correct as well as incorrect utterances and thus, the corrective goal embedded in the recast might be lost. Indeed, Nicholas, Lightbown, and Spada (2001) concluded that recasts seem to be effective only when it is clear to the learners that they are a reaction to the accuracy of the form of their utterances and not their content. Since this seems not to be the case for learners in content-based classes, several researchers have argued that explicit ways of making learners notice errors in their output are more effective.

Prompts, such as clarification requests, repetition of error, or metalinguistic clues not only ensure that learners notice the non-target form in their output, but also pushes them to repair output and to produce it accurately (Lyster, 2004; Panova & Lyster, 2002; Philp, 2003). Lyster (1998a, 1998b) suggests that prompts allow learners to retrieve acquired forms and practice them as a way to increase control. It seems, therefore, that learners in these classrooms have specific linguistic needs that recasts cannot fulfill. They might not so much need the input to be enhanced as a way to increase the noticing of a new form as they need opportunities to access and produce forms in the developing system as a way to increase control. It may be that recasts are more effective in non-content based L2 classrooms because learners are still at a stage in which they need the opportunity to process input for acquisition. In addition, they are less focused on content, and teachers can use recasts as an implicit corrective interactional strategy. In sum, classroom context appears to be one factor that moderates the effectiveness of corrective feedback as a pedagogical tool (see e.g., Sheen, 2004).

Context is not the only factor in determining the effectiveness of interactionally enhanced input. The roles of the initiator of the LRE and of the supplier of enhanced input have also been shown to be important. Ellis et al. (2001a) found that student-initiated episodes resulted in the most successful uptake. Williams (2001) found that learner-initiated LREs and LREs in which teachers responded to learner error resulted in similar levels of accuracy in post-tests. Both studies found teacher-initiated LREs to be the least effective. Regarding the supplier of the enhanced input during interaction (i.e., the learners themselves, the teacher, or another learner) proficiency seems to play an important role. Williams (2001) observed that post-test scores of low-proficiency learners was lower for forms supplied by other learners during LREs than for those supplied by the teacher. In contrast, the test scores of more advanced learners were similar regardless of who supplied the information during the LRE.

Limits on Interactional Enhancement of Input

As with any intervention, the success of enhancement in facilitating acquisition depends, in part, on factors external to the input itself. The most obvious limitation is in terms of pedagogical control. It is not always possible to predict which forms will require or get interactional enhancement, and it is almost impossible to predict the forms to which learners will attend during interaction. Interactional enhancement of input, therefore, is not a pedagogical technique that a teacher can easily use to target specific linguistic items.

Another limitation of interactional enhancement that we have already noted is the learners' stage of development. If learners do not notice interactionally enhanced forms, the enhancement will have little effect (Lyster, 1998a; Mackey, Gass, & McDonough, 2000; Nabei & Swain, 2001). Furthermore, even if learners do notice a form in the input during interaction, but are not able to attach meaning to it, it will not be processed and thus, will not become intake. For example, learners might become aware of a grammatical or lexical form used by the teacher or another learner but fail to map its meaning, either because it is not essential to the task or because the LRE is abandoned. Moreover, even if learners notice and process the enhanced input, but their developing systems are not able to accommodate the new information, the linguistic form will not be acquired. This phenomenon might explain, in part, why more advanced learners seem to benefit more from attention to form than do less advanced learners. Advanced learners can connect new forms to knowledge they have already acquired. This finding is robust, ranging from learner-learner LREs (Leesser, 2004; Williams, 2001), to recasts (Iwashita, 2003; Mackey & Philp, 1998). In sum, for input enhancement to be effective, learners need to be developmentally ready to notice, process, or accommodate it.

The effectiveness of enhancement may also be limited by the

nature of the task. If the learners are engaged in a task that is so cognitively demanding that they use all their attentional resources in order to perform it successfully, they are unlikely to attend to particular aspects of the input (Robinson, 2001; Skehan & Foster, 2001). Of course, a given task will make different demands on L2 learners of different levels of proficiency. Since attending to meaning during interaction is already complex and difficult for beginning L2 learners, a relatively simple task may take up all their attentional resources with little or none left to attend to form. This also may explain why advanced learners benefit more from input enhancement during interaction, and why they engage in more LREs than do low proficency learners (Leesser, 2004; Williams, 1999).

Finally, the effectiveness of the enhancement is related to the aspect of language that is in focus. Lyster has shown that phonological repairs tend to follow recasts whereas grammatical and lexical repairs tend to follow prompts or requests for clarification in content-based classrooms (1998a). Ellis et al. (2001a) also observed that successful uptake was more likely when the attention was drawn to problems in pronunciation than to problems in vocabulary. This may be because pronunciation problems are simply easier to repair, especially when a model is provided, as occurs in recasts. Numerous studies attest to the fact that learners focus on words before grammatical forms (Pica, 1994; VanPatten, 1996; Williams, 1999). Gass and Torres Alvarez (2005) report that learners in their study did not require enhancement of lexical items in order to notice them. In contrast, they often seemed to benefit from enhancement of grammatical aspects of the language. In fact, the findings on drawing learner attention to morphosyntactic forms is mixed. Research on negotiation suggests that learners rarely focus on these aspects of language during negotiation (Foster, 1998; Pica, 1992; Williams, 1999). In addition, learners have the most difficulty in noticing recasts of morphosyntactic errors, compared to feedback on pronunciation and lexical items (Mackey et al., 2000). Thus, it is important to distinguish among the aspects of language singled out for enhancement in any exploration of the effectiveness of interactionally modified input.

There are many different approaches to the study of second language acquisition and interaction plays a significant role in many of them. One recent review article on the topic of interaction states that the "links between interaction and learning have been clearly demonstrated" (Gass & Mackey, to appear). The enhancement of input can be one important outcome of interaction, affecting both the input itself and interlanguage processes. However, there are practical, cognitive, and developmental limits on its ultimate impact on learning.

Questions and Topics for Discussion

1) How do Williams and Fernández define input enhancement? How does this explanation differ from earlier definitions?
2) What is a *trigger*? Create a brief dialog (specifically an LRE) that contains an example of a trigger.
3) What is positive and negative evidence? Provide an example of each.
4) Discuss the notions of *noticing, comprehension,* and *uptake* and the relationships thereof.
5) Discuss the limitations of interactional enhancement.
6) Create a short dialog containing an example of interactionally enhanced input and successful uptake.

Notes

Unless otherwise noted, all data come from classroom interaction recorded by the first author for a larger study in 1999.

References

Ayoun, D. (2001). The role of positive and negative feedback in the second language acquisition of the *passé composé* and *imparfait. Modern Language Journal, 85,* 226-243.

Ayoun, D. (2004). The effectiveness of written recasts in the second language acquisition of aspectual distinctions in French: A follow-up study. *Modern Language Journal, 88,* 31-55.

Barcroft, J., & VanPatten, B. (1997). Acoustic salience of grammatical forms: The effect of location, stress, and boundedness on Spanish L2 input processing. In A.T. Pérez-Leroux & W.R. Glass (Eds.), *Contemporary perspectives on the acquisition of Spanish: Vol 2. Production, processing, and comprehension* (pp. 109-121). Somerville, MA: Cascadilla Press.

Basturkmen, H., Loewen, S., & Ellis, R. (2001). Metalanguage in focus on form in the communicative classroom. *Language Awareness, 11,* 1-13.

de la Fuente, M.J. (2002). Negotiation and oral acquisition of L2 vocabulary: The roles of input and output in receptive and productive acquisition of words. *Studies in Second Language Acquisition, 24,* 81-112.

Doughty, C., & Varela, E. (1998). Communicative focus on form. In C. Doughty & J. Williams (Eds.), *Focus on form in classroom second language acquisition* (pp. 114-138). Cambridge: Cambridge University Press.

Doughty, C., & Williams, J. (1998). Pedagogical choices in focus on form. In C. Doughty & J. Williams (Eds.), *Focus on form in classroom second language acquisition* (pp. 197-261). Cambridge: Cambridge University Press.

Ellis, R. (1999). Theoretical perspectives on interaction and language learning. In R. Ellis (Ed.), *Learning a second language through interaction* (pp. 3-31). Amsterdam: Benjamins.

Ellis, R. (2001). Investigating form-focused instruction. *Language Learning, 51*, Supplement 1, 1-46.

Ellis, R., Basturkmen, H., & Loewen, S. (2001a). Learner uptake in communicative ESL lessons. *Language Learning, 51*, 281-318.

Ellis, R., Basturkmen, H., & Loewen, S. (2001b). Preemptive focus on form in the ESL classroom. *TESOL Quarterly, 35,* 407-432.

Ellis, R., Tanaka, Y., & Yamazaki, A. (1994). Classroom interaction, comprehension, and the acquisition of L2 word meanings. *Language Learning, 44,* 449-491.

Foster, P. (1998). A classroom perspective on the negotiation of meaning. *Applied Linguistics, 19,* 1-23.

Foster, P., & Ohta, A. (2005). Negotiation for meaning and peer assistance in second language classrooms. *Applied Linguistics, 26,* 402-430.

Gass, S. (1997). *Input, interaction, and the second language learner.* Mahwah, NJ: Lawrence Erlbaum.

Gass, S., & Mackey, A. (to appear). Input, interaction, and output in second language acquisition. In B. VanPatten & J. Williams (Eds.), *Theories in second language acquisition.* Mahwah, NJ: Lawrence Erlbaum.

Gass, S., & Torres Alvarez, M. (2005). Attention when? An investigation of the ordering effect of input and interaction. *Studies in Second Language Acquisition, 27,* 1-31.

Han, Z.H. (2002). A study of the impact of recasts on tense consistency in L2 output. *TESOL Quarterly, 36,* 543-572.

Iwashita, N. (2003). Negative feedback and positive evidence in task-based interaction: Differential effects on L2 development. *Studies in Second Language Acquisition, 25,* 1-36.

Klein, W. (1986). *Second language acquisition.* Cambridge: Cambridge University Press.

Krashen, S. (1985). *The input hypothesis: Issues and implications.* Torrance, CA: Laredo Publishing Company, Inc.

Leeman, J. (2003). Recasts and second language development: Beyond negative evidence. *Studies in Second Language Acquisition, 25,* 37-63.

Leesser, M. (2004). Learner proficiency and focus on form during collaborative dialogue. *Language Teaching Research, 8,* 55-81.

Loewen, S. (2003). Variation in the frequency and characteristics of incidental focus on form. *Language Teaching Research, 7,* 315-345.

Loewen, S. (2004). Uptake in incidental focus on form in meaning-focused ESL lessons. *Language Learning, 54,* 153-187.

Loewen, S. (2005). Incidental focus on form and second language learning. *Studies in Second Language Acquisition, 27,* 361-386.

Long, M.H., Inagaki, S., & Ortega, L. (1998). The role of implicit negative feedback in SLA: Models and recasts in Japanese and Spanish. *Modern Language Journal, 82,* 357-71.

Loschky, L. (1994). Comprehensible input and second language acquisition. What is the relationship? *Studies in Second Language Acquisition, 19,* 37-66.

Lyster, R. (1998a). Negotiation of form, recasts, and explicit correction in relation to error types and learner repair in immersion classrooms. *Language Learning, 48,* 183-218.

Lyster, R. (1998b). Recasts, repetition, and ambiguity in L2 classroom discourse. *Studies in Second Language Acquisition, 20,* 51-80.

Lyster, R. (2004). Differential effects of prompts and recasts in form-focused interaction. *Studies in Second Language Acquisition, 26,* 399-432.

Lyster, R., & Ranta, L. (1997). Corrective feedback and learner uptake: Negotiation of form in communicative classrooms. *Studies in Second Language Acquisition, 19,* 37-66.

Mackey, A. (1999). Input, interaction and second language development: An empirical study of question formation in ESL. *Studies in Second Language Acquisition, 21,* 557-587.

Mackey, A., Gass, S., & McDonough, K. (2000). How do learners perceive interactional feedback? *Studies in Second Language Acquisition, 22,* 471-497.

Mackey, A., & Philp, J. (1998). Recasts, interaction, and interlanguage development: Are responses red herrings? *Modern Language Journal, 82,* 338-356.

Muranoi, H. (2000). Focus on form through interaction enhancement: Integrating formal instruction into a communicative task in EFL classrooms. *Language Learning, 50,* 617-673.

Nabei, T., & Swain, M. (2001). Learner awareness of recasts in classroom interaction: A case study of an adult EFL student's second language learning. *Language Awareness, 11,* 43-63.

Neisser, U. (1967). *Cognitive psychology.* New York: Appleton.

Nicholas, H., Lightbown, P., & Spada, N. (2001). Recasts as feedback to language learners. *Language Learning, 51,* 719-758.

Nobuyoshi, J., & Ellis, R. (1993). Focused communication tasks and second language acquisition. *ELT Journal, 47,* 203-210.

Ohta, A. (2000). Rethinking recasts: A learner-centered examination of corrective feedback in the Japanese language classroom. In J. K. Hall & L. Verplaetse (Eds.), *Second and foreign language learning through classroom interaction* (pp. 47-71). Mahwah, NJ: Lawrence Erlbaum.

Oliver, R. (1995). Negative feedback in child NS-NNS conversation. *Studies in Second Language Acquisition, 17,* 459-482.

Panova, I., & Lyster, R. (2002). Patterns of corrective feedback and uptake in the adult ESL classroom. *TESOL Quarterly, 36,* 573-595.

Philp. J. (2003). Constraints on "Noticing the gap": Nonnative speakers' noticing of recasts in NS-NNS interaction. *Studies in Second Language Acquisition, 25,* 99- 126.

Pica, T. (1992). The textual outcomes of native speaker-non-native speaker negotiation: What do they reveal about second language learning? In C. Kramsch & S. McConnell-Ginet (Eds.), *Text and context* (pp. 198-237). Cambridge, MA: D.C. Heath.

Pica, T. (1994). Research on negotiation: What does it reveal about second language acquisition? *Language Learning, 44,* 493-527.

Pica, T. (2002). Subject-matter content: How does it assist the interactional and linguistic needs of classroom language learners? *Modern Language Journal, 86,* 1-19.

Pica, T., Doughty, C., & Young, R. (1986). Making input comprehensible: Do interactional modifications help? *ITL Review of Applied Linguistics, 72,* 1-25.

Pica, T., Young, R., & Doughty, C. (1987). The impact of interaction on comprehension. *TESOL Quarterly, 21,* 737-758.

Robinson, P. (1995). Review article: Attention, memory, and the noticing hypothesis. *Language Learning, 45,* 283-331.

Robinson, R. (2001). Task complexity, cognitive resources and syllabus design: A triadic framework for examining task influences on SLA. In P. Robinson (Ed.), *Cognition and second language instruction* (pp. 287-318). Cambridge: Cambridge University Press.

Schmidt, R. (1995). Consciousness and foreign language learning. In R. Schmidt (Ed.), *Attention and awareness in foreign language learning,* (pp. 1-63). Honolulu: University of Hawai'i Press.

Schmidt, R. (2001). Attention. In P. Robinson (Ed.), *Cognition and second language instruction* (pp. 3-32). Cambridge: Cambridge University Press.

Schmidt, R., & Frota, S. (1986). Developing basic conversational ability in a second language. In R. Day (Ed.), *Talking to learn* (pp. 237-326). Rowley, MA: Newbury House.

Sharwood Smith, M. (1981). Conscious raising and the second language learner. *Applied Linguistics, 2*, 159-168.

Sheen, Y. (2004). Corrective feedback and learner uptake in communicative classrooms across instructional settings. *Language Teaching Research, 8*, 263-300.

Shehadeh, A. (1999). Non-native speakers' production of modified comprehensible output and second language learning. *Language Learning, 49*, 627-675.

Shehadeh, A. (2001). Self- and other-initiated modified output during task-based interaction. *TESOL Quarterly, 35*, 433-457.

Skehan, P., & Foster, P. (2001). Cognition and tasks. In P. Robinson (Ed.), *Cognition and second language instruction* (pp. 183-205). Cambridge: Cambridge University Press.

Swain, M. (1995). Three functions of output in second language learning. In G. Cook & B. Seidlhofer (Eds.), *Principle and practice in applied linguistics* (pp. 125-144). Oxford: Oxford University Press.

White, J. (1998). Getting the learners' attention: A typographical input enhancement study. In C. Doughty & J. Williams (Eds.), *Focus on form in classroom second language acquisition* (pp. 85-113). Cambridge: Cambridge University Press.

VanPatten, B. (1990). Attending to form and content in the input: An experiment in consciousness. *Studies in Second Language Acquisition, 12*, 287-301.

VanPatten, B. (1996). *Input processing and grammar instruction.* New York: Ablex.

Williams, J. (1999). Learner-generated attention to form. *Language Learning, 49*, 583- 625.

Williams, J. (2001). The effectiveness of spontaneous attention to form. *System, 29*, 325- 340.

Wong, W. (2003). The effects of textual enhancement and simplified input on L2 comprehension and acquisition of non-meaningful grammatical form. *Applied Language Learning, 14*, 109-132.

Wong, W. (2005). *Input enhancement. From theory and research to the classroom.* New York: McGraw Hill.

Chapter 8
Complementary Roles for Input and Output Enhancement in Form-Focused Instruction

Roy Lyster, McGill University

The aim of this chapter is to provide empirical support from classroom-based research that illustrates, first, an important role for input enhancement in form-focused instruction and, second, an equally important and complementary role for output enhancement.

Form-focused instruction, according to Ellis (2001, pp. 1-2), refers to "any planned or incidental instructional activity that is intended to induce language learners to pay attention to linguistic form" (see also Spada, 1997). A great deal of research pertaining to form-focused instruction has been undertaken in the context of immersion classrooms. **Immersion** is a type of content-based instruction in which students receive part of their subject-matter instruction through the medium of a second or foreign language and part through their first language (Genesee, 1987). This innovation was based on the rationale that young children are naturally predisposed to learn additional languages through early exposure in message-oriented contexts (Lambert & Tucker, 1972).

Given its predominant focus on meaning, immersion provides a rich context for research into innovative ways of teaching and learning a second language. Immersion classrooms replicate conditions for sustained exposure and authentic communication more than most other instructional settings insofar as the target language is used purposefully for the study of other subjects. In this sense, immersion provides, theoretically at least, a classroom context with optimal conditions for second language learning. In terms of learning outcomes, research has indeed shown that immersion students develop high levels of comprehension skills as well as considerable fluency and confidence in second language production. However, these studies also point to shortcomings in grammatical accuracy that persist in immersion students' interlanguage development even after years of immersion education (Harley, Cummins, Swain, & Allen, 1990). Immersion education thus provides a clear example of an instructional context where focus on meaningful content leads to the development of overall communicative ability, but with linguistic gaps in terms of accuracy.

Imagine that you are a sixth-grade immersion student listening to your teacher give the following description of late 18th-century life in the Antilles in your second language:

> How do you think these plantations ... are going ... to change ... life in the Antilles? [...] These people are going to sell their sugar, rum, molasses, brown sugar. They are going to make money. With the money, they are going to buy clothes, furniture, horses, carriages ... all they want and they are going to bring them back to the Antilles (Swain, 1996, p. 533).

Even though this is a history lesson about events that took place more than 200 years ago, did you notice that the teacher uses the immediate future tense to convey her message? Swain describes the teacher's choice of tense as "superb from a content teaching point of view" (p.533). Indeed, the passage brought the distant past "into the lives of the children, got them involved, and undoubtedly helped them to understand the social and economic principle that this historical unit was intended to demonstrate. However, as a language lesson modeling past tense usage, it was less than a success" (Swain, 1996, p. 533).

Swain (1985, 1988, 1996) has argued convincingly that content teaching, because it generates functionally restricted input, is not, on its own, good language teaching. For example, again with respect to verb tenses, Swain reported the findings of a classroom observation study that revealed that 75% of all verbs used by immersion teachers were restricted to present tense or imperative forms, whereas only 15%

were in the past tense, 6% were in the future tense, and 3% were in the conditional mood. Other language features appear more frequently in immersion classroom input (e.g., grammatical gender markers) but are not salient or meaningful enough for students to actually notice (Harley, 1993). Therefore, as succinctly captured by the title of her seminal article, Swain (1988) argued that content teaching needs to be manipulated and complemented in ways that will maximize second language learning. Drawing on research conducted in immersion classrooms with her colleagues (e.g., Harley, Allen, Cummins, & Swain, 1990), Swain proposed that situations must be developed to ensure that students both "hear and read the language we want them to learn, and to ensure that students are given opportunities to be *pushed* beyond their current abilities in the target language through the provision of feedback on the accuracy, coherence and appropriateness of the immersion language they use" (Swain, 1996, p. 545).

Complementing language used for content teaching in this way points to an important role for input enhancement, which, according to Sharwood Smith (1993), teachers can manipulate in ways that create either positive or negative input enhancement. **Positive input enhancement** is intended to make certain forms more salient in the input, through color coding or boldfacing in the case of written input, and through intonational stress and gestures in the case of oral input. **Negative input enhancement** is intended to flag certain forms as incorrect, primarily through the use of corrective feedback.

The remainder of this chapter illustrates how teachers can effectively incorporate both positive and negative input enhancement into form-focused instructional interventions that are either proactive or reactive (Doughty & Williams, 1998; Lyster, 1998b; Rebuffot & Lyster, 1996). Also suggested in this chapter is that input enhancement is best implemented in conjunction with a range of metalinguistic tasks and practice activities that include opportunities for "output enhancement" (Takashima & Ellis, 1999). Although all examples of classroom interaction in this chapter are extracted from immersion settings, readers with an interest in non-immersion programs are reminded of the relevance of immersion pedagogy to other second language instructional settings, as expounded in Genesee's (1991) 'lessons from immersion': namely, that effective second language pedagogy, irrespective of instructional setting, strives for integration of language and content, extensive interaction, and systematic planning for language development.

Positive Input Enhancement

Positive input enhancement can be implemented through a proactive instructional approach, which involves planned form-focused instruction designed to enable students to notice and use second language features that would otherwise not be used or even noticed. Proactive form-focused instruction is generally considered most effective when embedded in communicative activities and is thus different from traditional grammar lessons, which emphasize the learning and categorizing of forms out of context and that appear to have minimal effect in classrooms where learners' exposure to the second language has been primarily message-oriented (Swain, 1996). A series of experimental studies undertaken in French immersion classrooms demonstrated that a proactive instructional approach can benefit students' interlanguage development, in varying degrees, in areas known to be difficult for classroom learners of French as a second language: namely, aspect (Harley, 1989), the conditional mood (Day & Shapson, 1991), sociostylistic variation (Lyster, 1994a), verbs of motion (Wright, 1996), and grammatical gender (Harley, 1998; Lyster, 2004). Instructional treatments in these studies used input enhancement to promote the perception of problematic target features in a variety of genres (e.g., curriculum materials, legends, letters, invitations, novels, songs, rhyming verses) and through language games including Bingo, Concentration, Simon Says, crossword puzzles, and word searches.

An optional feature of positive input enhancement is the extent to which the enhanced input is accompanied by or followed by some type of elaboration, ranging from inductive rule-discovery tasks to deductive metalinguistic explanations (Sharwood Smith, 1981, 1993). For example, the teachers in Lyster's (2004) study used typographically enhanced input to draw fifth-graders' attention to grammatical gender in French by boldfacing, throughout the students' curriculum materials, the endings of nouns that reliably predict their gender. Students were then asked to group together nouns with similar endings and determine which gender their endings predict; this is an example of a rule-discovery task following exposure to enhanced input. Similarly, in Harley's (1989) study of the effects of form-focused instruction on the acquisition of perfective and imperfective past tenses in French, students began by reading a traditional legend about were-wolves. The legend had been enhanced in the sense that past tense forms occurred frequently and the functional distinctions between the two tenses were made salient by the narrative. Then students were asked to identify the two different past tenses in the text and, based on the narrative, to infer the different functions of each tense. In yet another classroom intervention study in French immersion classrooms, Day and Shapson (1991) investigated the effects of instruction on seventh-graders' use of the conditional in French. One of the games required students to choose the correct hypothetical outcome in a series of experiments, an example of which follows:

Voici un ballon gonflé. Si vous le mettiez au frigidaire toute la nuit, que se passerait-il?	Here is an inflated balloon. If you put it in the refrigerator over night, what would happen?
(a) le ballon grossirait	(a) the balloon would expand
(b) le ballon repetisserait	(b) the balloon would deflate
(c) le ballon éclaterait	(c) the balloon would pop

    Increasing the frequency of the conditional in this way is a type of positive input enhancement that makes the form more salient. But enhancing input so that students are more likely to notice target forms is only the first step. In addition, teachers provided metalinguistic information that drew students' attention to the fact that the conditional is used to express hypotheses and other possible yet uncertain outcomes in the future.

    Without some follow-up elaboration that includes rule-discovery tasks or the provision of metalinguistic information, input enhancement alone is likely insufficient as a pedagogical intervention. For example, in her study of the effects of typographical input enhancement on the acquisition of possessive determiners by francophone learners of English, White (1998) concluded that the sixth-graders in her study would have benefited from more explicit information than that made available through enhanced input alone. Similarly, in her study of the effects of instruction on the acquisition of past tenses in French, Harley (1989) concluded that students would have made more significant progress had they been provided with metalinguistic information about the formal properties of the two tenses.

    In any case, it remains difficult and time-consuming for immersion and other content-based language teachers to produce, on a regular basis, engaging materials that aptly employ input enhancement to make target features more salient. What teachers have more control over is the oral input they provide during teacher-student interaction. The next section focuses on how teachers can use input enhancement to manipulate their use of the target language as they exploit one of the most powerful tools for learning a second language: interaction.

Classroom Interaction

Interaction plays a key role in driving second language development forward, according to Long's (1996) interaction hypothesis, because a primary source of positive and negative data (i.e., what is possible and not possible to say in the target language) is made available to learners during meaningful interaction with a more competent speaker. Interaction also provides learners with opportunities to control the input to some extent, as they ask their interlocutor to modify his or her speech in ways that make the input more accessible and more likely to be integrated into the learners' developing interlanguage system (Gass, 1997; Long, 1996; Pica, 1994).

In second language classrooms, teacher-student interaction provides propitious opportunities for reactive focus on form to occur in relatively unplanned ways that include teacher feedback that targets students' non-target output. Research in support of reactive focus on form suggests that it may be precisely at the moment when students have something to say that their attention can most effectively be drawn to form, rather than postponing attention to form until a subsequent language lesson (Lightbown, 1991, 1998; Long, 1991). Observational studies of French immersion classrooms have provided detailed descriptions of how teachers interact with students and use a range of questioning techniques and feedback types to draw attention to form during language arts and science lessons (Lapkin & Swain, 1996; Laplante, 1993; Lyster, 1994b, 1998b).

In second language acquisition research, interactional moves that facilitate comprehension while potentially drawing attention to form are often referred to as 'negotiation' or 'negotiated interaction.' In classroom settings, it has proven useful to distinguish between the negotiation of meaning and the negotiation of form (Lyster, 2002). Doing so allows educators to appreciate the different discourse functions entailed in negotiating for meaning and negotiating for form, and their differential roles in facilitating input enhancement versus output enhancement.

Recasts as Negative Input Enhancement

Negotiation of meaning has been operationalized as a set of conversational moves used in dyadic interaction. According to Long (1996), negotiation of meaning comprises the following types of interactional features:
- input modifications (e.g., stress on key words, decomposition, partial self-repetition);
- semantically contingent responses (e.g., recasts, repetition, expansions);
- conversational modifications (e.g., confirmations, confirmation checks, comprehension checks, clarification requests).

These interactional features are hypothesized to provide second language learners with a primary source of **negative evidence** (i.e., information about ungrammaticality) in ways that benefit second language development. One type of semantically contingent feedback that figures in Long's (1996) taxonomy of negotiation of meaning strategies, and that has received increasing attention in both first and second language contexts, is the **recast**—a well-formed reformulation of a learner utterance with the original meaning intact. Recasts are by far the most frequently used feedback in a range of classroom settings: elementary immersion classrooms (Lyster & Ranta, 1997; Mori, 2002), university-level foreign language classrooms (Doughty, 1994; Roberts, 1995), high school English as a foreign language (EFL) classrooms (Tsang, 2004), and adult ESL classrooms (Ellis, Basturkmen, & Loewen, 2001; Panova & Lyster, 2002).

As defined in the first language acquisition literature and as observed in French immersion classrooms, recasting (i.e., an implicit target-like reformulation of a learner's utterance) may not be the most effective way of enhancing input for the purpose of drawing young second language learners' attention to form. Lyster (1998a) illustrated that recasts, which are used frequently by French immersion teachers to respond to students' ill-formed utterances, compete with a similar proportion of teacher repetitions of well-formed utterances. Recasts of ill-formed utterances and repetitions of well-formed utterances together appear to confirm or disconfirm the content or veracity, not the form, of a student's message. Adding to the ambiguity is the frequent use of signs of approval as positive feedback following student utterances, irrespective of accuracy, including affirmations such as *oui, c'est ça,* and *O.K.*, and praise markers such as *Très bien, Bravo,* and *Excellent* (Lyster, 1998a). A closer look at interaction in a social studies lesson will illustrate the consequent ambiguity from the second language learner's perspective.

The following examples are extracted from a science lesson about the water cycle taught by Marie, who draws on negotiation of meaning strategies to present content to her 9-10-year-old fourth-grade mid-immersion students.

Example 8.1[1]

1) T:	*Qu'est-ce que c'est un ruisseau encore? [...] Oui?*	1) T:	What's a stream again? [...] Yes?
2) S:	*C'est comme un petit lac.*	2) S:	It's like a small lake.
3) T:	*Un petit lac qu'on a dit?*	3) T:	A small lake we said?
4) S1:	*C'est *un petit* rivière.*	4) S1:	It's a small [wrong gender] river.
5) T:	*C'est ça. C'est plus une petite rivière, O.K.? Parce qu'un lac c'est comme un endroit où il y a de l'eau mais c'est un...?*	5) T:	That's it It's more like a little river, O.K.? Because a lake is a place where there's water but it's a ...
6) Ss:	*Comme un cercle.*	6) Ss:	Like a circle.
7) T:	*C'est comme un cercle [...]. Puis là elle se retrouve près d'une fôret. Et qu'est-ce qu'ils font dans la forêt? Will?*	7) T:	It's like a circle [...]. And so she finds herself near a forest. And what do they do in the forest? Will?
8) S2:	*Ils coupent des arbres.*	8) S2:	They cut down trees.
9) T:	*Ils coupent des arbres. Et quand on coupe des arbres et qu'on est en plein milieu de la fôret, est-ce qu'on peut amener un camion puis mettre le bois dedans? Y a pas toujours un chemin pour faire cela. Qu'est-ce qu'on fait pour transporter le bois?*	9) T:	They cut down trees. And when you cut down trees and you're in the middle of the forest, can you bring a truck to put the wood in? There's not always a road for that. What do they do to transport the wood?
10) S3:	*Euh, tu mets le bois dans l'eau et les euhm... comment dis tu euh [carries]?*	10) S3:	Um, you put the wood in the water and the um, how do you say /carries/?
11) Ss:	*Emporte.*	11) Ss:	'Emporte.'
12) T:	*Emporte, bien.*	12) T:	Emporte, good.
13) S3:	**Emporte le arbre au un place puis un autre personne qui met le bois.**	13) S3:	*Carries [] tree to an place and another person who puts the wood.*
14) T:	*C'est ça. Alors, on met le bois dans la rivière pour qu'il soit transporté d'un endroit à l'autre.*	14) T:	That's it. So, they put the wood in the river so it gets transported from one place to another.

Marie begins by asking students what a *ruisseau* or a stream is. She repeats the first student's response (*un petit lac*) in a confirmation check in line 3 to disconfirm this incorrect yet well-formed response. The next student's answer (*un petit rivière*) is correct in terms of content although the grammatical gender is incorrect. Marie approves the content with *c'est ça* and then unobtrusively modifies the gender in her recast before asking more about how a lake differs from a river. Notice her exact repetition in line 9 of Will's response, *Ils coupent des arbres*, which is accurate both in form and meaning. Next is a good example of collective scaffolding as a student in line 10 tries to describe how the wood is transported, but needs to ask how to say 'carries' in French. His classmates respond in line 11 with *emporte*, which allows him to continue in line 13 with an ill-formed utterance: *Emporte le arbre au un place puis un autre personne qui met le bois*. This is met with approval in line 14 (*C'est ça*), despite its ill-formedness, because Marie understands what the student is trying to say, as is made clear in her subsequent recast. The subject matter here is complex for these fourth-graders, and this exchange is a good example of scaffolding on Marie's part that allows students to express ideas that they would not be able to express on their own. As a result of various repetitions and reformulations, the input is enhanced in ways that make it comprehensible but not deliberately enhanced so that it draws attention to discrepancies between her input and the students' output.

Some researchers uphold recasts as a type of feedback of prime importance, hypothesized to trigger noticing and thereby promote second language development (e.g., Doughty, 2001; Long, 1996; Long & Robinson, 1998). For example, Doughty (2001) argued that recasting is an ideal type of feedback, because second language learners are able to store the target reformulation in working memory and make a cognitive comparison between input and output. However, according to de Bot (2000), "there is never a direct comparison between input and output because the input information is immediately processed and not stored in memory in that form" (p. 228). Sharwood Smith (1993), arguing in support of input enhancement, also stressed that learners are able to process input for meaning alone (see also VanPatten, 1990), without noticing and storing reformulated target forms in a way that changes their interlanguage system. For recasts to serve as input enhancement, students need, first, to know that their output was indeed non-target-like and, second, intentionally hold the non-target-like utterance in memory long enough to make a cognitive comparison with the enhanced input. At least three classroom studies have demonstrated the effectiveness of recasts when their saliency in classroom input is enhanced to facilitate such input-output comparisons.

In two classroom studies with young adult learners of French as a foreign language, Tomasello and Herron (1988, 1989) investigated the effects of feedback provided during teacher-led drills. In response to a set of transfer and overgeneralization errors that students were led to produce orally, the teacher first wrote the incorrect form on the chalkboard, then provided a recast orally and also wrote the correct form on the chalkboard. Both studies showed clear benefits for this type of explicit error treatment. The researchers designed the pedagogical intervention to include correct and incorrect forms written on the chalkboard, in addition to oral recasts, in order to allow time for visual and cognitive comparison. Tomasello and Herron (1989) concluded that "recasts do not seem to work in the L2 classroom" because "students in a classroom context believe that a teacher's positive response indicates that no correction is needed" (p. 392). A similar attempt to make recasts appear salient was apparent in Doughty and Varela's (1998) study of two multilevel (5th to 8th grade) content-based ESL classrooms. In the experimental classroom, students received feedback on simple past and conditional past tense forms during science activities. The other class engaged in the same science activities but without feedback. Two types of feedback—together called **corrective recasting**—were used in sequence. First, the teacher repeated the student's non-target utterance, drawing attention to the error with stress and rising intonation; second, if the learner failed to respond, the teacher provided a recast in which the verb form was stressed.

Without such deliberate enhancement intended to contrast target and non-target forms, recasts used more naturalistically may fall short of providing students with sufficiently enhanced input. Even if students did notice the enhanced input provided in a teacher's recast, they might infer that the recast is simply a different, but not better, way of saying the same thing. French immersion students participating in the preceding exchange about the water cycle could infer that gender attribution in French is simply random and results from free variation because, according to their classroom input, *rivière* can be either masculine or feminine. That is, their teacher responded to the non-target *C'est un petit rivière* with an affirmation (*C'est ça*) to confirm the veracity of the content, without any noticeable disapproval in her subsequent recast.

We see this again in Example 2 where Marie's question about Perlette elicits two responses, each of which contains well-known errors in French as a second language.

Example 8.2

1) T:	[...] Pourquoi est-ce qu'elle veut se faire réchauffer vous pensez? Oui?	1) T:	[...] Why does she want to warm up do you think? Yes?
2) S:	Parce qu'elle *est* trop froid pour aller dans toutes les [?]	2) S:	Because she *has* too cold to go into all the [?]
3) T:	Parce qu'elle a trop froid, O.K. Oui?	3) T:	Because she is too cold, O.K. Yes?
4) S1:	Elle *est* trop peur.	4) S1:	She *has* too frightened.
5) T:	Parce qu'elle a peur, oui.	5) T:	Because she is frightened, yes.

The first response in line 2 (*parce qu'elle est trop froid*) is followed by a recast in line 3 (*parce qu'elle a trop froid*) as well as by the approval marker *O.K.* The next non-target utterance in line 4 (*elle est trop peur*) is also followed by a recast in line 5 as well as by a sign of approval, *Oui*. Given that *avoir* and *être* distinctions are known to be confusing to immersion students, as documented for example by Harley (1993), recasts provided as implicitly as this may be particularly ambiguous and may even confirm that the two forms are interchangeable.

In many other classroom settings, however, studies have shown that recasts are indeed noticed by students insofar as they lead to immediate student repetition. Whereas infrequent repair following recasts has been observed in French immersion classrooms (Lyster & Ranta, 1997), adult ESL in Canada (Panova & Lyster, 2002), and EFL in Hong Kong secondary schools (Tsang, 2004), more frequent repair following recasts has been observed in Japanese immersion classrooms (Mori, 2002), adult ESL classrooms in New Zealand (Ellis et al., 2001), and adult EFL conversational classes in Korea (Sheen, 2004). These discrepant findings led Lyster and Mori (2006) to do a comparative study of French and Japanese immersion classrooms to gain a better understanding of the contextual variables that make recasts more noticeable and more likely to be repeated in Japanese immersion classrooms than in French immersion classrooms. The study compared patterns of corrective feedback and learner repair in four French immersion classrooms in Canada and three Japanese immersion classrooms in the US, all at the fourth- or fifth-grade level. We used two coding schemes to compare the instructional settings. First, we used Lyster and Ranta's (1997) error treatment model to identify specific patterns of interactional feedback and learner uptake. Second, we used Spada and Fröhlich's (1995) Communicative Orientation to Language Teaching (COLT) coding scheme to identify similarities and differences in other instructional variables across the two settings. Part A of the COLT scheme allowed us to observe and code pedagogical activities according to participant organization (whole class, group, individual), content (procedural, linguistic, thematic), content control (teacher, student, text), and student modality (listening, speaking, reading, writing).

Measuring the effectiveness of feedback in terms of its propensity to lead to immediate repair, we confirmed that recasts were more effective in Japanese immersion classrooms, where students accurately repeated 50% of all recasts, than in French immersion classrooms, where students accurately repeated only 19% of all recasts. We attributed the effectiveness of recasts at eliciting more student repair in Japanese to two instructional design features that were observed only in the Japanese classrooms: (a) the use of choral repetition and (b) an emphasis on speaking as a skill practiced in isolation through repetition and reading aloud. We detected an emphasis in Japanese classrooms on accurate oral production, apparent in various activities involving repetition of teacher models, which likely served to prime Japanese immersion students for repeating their teachers' recasts. We concluded that recasts are generally more effective in form-focused classrooms than in meaning-focused classrooms (see also Nicholas, Lightbown, & Spada, 2001), and that this is also the case even in content-based classrooms that provide regular opportunities for controlled production practice with an emphasis on accuracy. In particular, classroom activities that include choral and other types of repetition are likely to bias learners' attention toward form in ways that predispose them to notice the corrective function of recasts. Example 3 illustrates a student's repetition of a recast during a social studies lesson in a Japanese immersion classroom (Lyster & Mori, 2006).

Example 8.3

1) S:	Basha o irete to, um, um, trail ni mottearimasu.	1) S:	They put the wagon in it and, um, um, have had it to the trail.
2) T:	Ikimasu, motteikimasu.	2) T:	They go, they take it to the trail.
3) S:	Motteikimasu.	3) S:	They take it to the trail.
4) T:	Basha no naka ni irete trail ni motteiku. Dakara ie no naka ni okimasen. Wakaru?	4) T:	They put it in the wagon and take it to the trail. So they don't put it in the house. Do you understand?

In this exchange, not only does the student, in line 3, repeat the teacher's recast from line 2, but the teacher then reformulates the student's first turn, which included several errors, in its entirety. Compare this with the exchange in Example 4 from one of the French immersion classrooms (Lyster & Mori, 2006).

Example 8.4

1) S:	Nous sommes allés au Biodôme parce que ma grand-mère elle *a jamais allé à là- bas.*	1) S:	We went to the Biodome because my grandmother *never goed to there.*
2) T:	Elle était jamais allée.	2) T:	She had never gone.
3) S:	Puis on *a* allé à /Jungle Adventure/ et on a gagné des prix.	3) S:	Then we *goed* to Jungle Adventure and we won prizes.
4) T:	C'est quoi ça?	4) T:	What is that ?

After the teacher's recast in line 2, the student simply continues in line 3 recounting his March Break activities without repeating the recast. Not only does the student not repeat the teacher's recast but he makes a similar error in line 3, which the teacher ignores and instead asks the student in line 4 to elaborate on the content of his message. Arguably, the teacher's recast in Japanese in Example 3, because the student immediately repeats it, served more effectively as input enhancement than the teacher's recast in French, which the student appears to ignore in Example 4. However, we found that other types of feedback, discussed in the next section under the rubric of prompts, proved to be equally effective in both instructional settings.

Prompting for Output Enhancement

As we saw in Marie's lesson about the water cycle, mutual comprehension can easily be achieved in classroom interaction, despite students' use of non-target forms. For this reason, Swain (1985) argued that teachers, in order to benefit their students' interlanguage development, need to incorporate ways of "pushing" students to produce language that is not only comprehensible, but also accurate. In Lyster and Ranta (1997), we identified four interactional moves that teachers use to push learners to improve the accuracy of their non-target output:

- **Clarification request**: the teacher indicates to the student, by using phrases such as "*Pardon me*" and "*I don't understand*," that the

message has not been understood or that the utterance is ill-formed in some way.
- **Repetition**: the teacher repeats the student's erroneous utterance, adjusting the intonation to highlight the error.
- **Metalinguistic clues**: the teacher provides comments, information, or questions related to the well-formedness of the student's utterance, without explicitly providing the correct form (e.g., *"Do we say 'goed' in English?" "Ça se dit pas en français," "Non, pas ça," "Is it masculine?"*).
- **Elicitation**: the teacher directly elicits correct forms from students by asking questions such as *"Comment ça s'appelle?"* or *"How do we say that in French?"*; or by pausing to allow students to complete the teacher's utterance (e.g., *"C'est un... "*); or by asking students to reformulate their utterance (e.g., *"Try again"*).

Although these four prompting moves, used separately or in combination, represent a wide range of feedback types, they have one crucial feature in common that distinguishes them from recasts: they withhold correct forms and instead offer learners an opportunity to self-repair by generating their own modified response. Thus, whereas recasts potentially serve as input enhancement in some classroom settings, especially those with a form-focused orientation, prompts lead to what Takashima and Ellis (1999) call "output enhancement." **Output enhancement** is the desired effect of prompting moves, both in the short- and long-term: namely, more accurate output that has been enhanced or modified relative to the learner's initially erroneous utterance. Open-ended feedback signals that tend to lead to output enhancement (see Pica, Lincoln-Porter, Paninos, & Linnell, 1996) have been referred to elsewhere as **negotiation of form** (e.g., Lyster, 1998a; Lyster & Ranta, 1997), but are referred to here as **prompts** (see Lyster, 2004; Lyster & Mori, 2006; Ranta & Lyster, 2006) in order to avoid confusion with negotiation of meaning strategies that aim primarily for message comprehensibility rather than formal accuracy (e.g., Long, 1996; Pica, 1994).

The examples that follow are extracted from two different fourth-grade classrooms where the interaction concerns what students did during their March Break. In Example 5, a student describes a shopping expedition with his grandmother to his teacher, Rachelle.

Example 8.5

1) S:	Pis euhm, *j'ai allé* au mall	1) S:	And, um, I *goed* to the mall…
…			
2) T:	"J'ai allé" ça ne se dit pas.	2) T:	"I goed," we don't say that.
3) S:	Je suis allé au mall de St-Benoît et j'ai…	3) S:	I went to the St-Benoit mall and I …
4) T:	Tu as acheté quelque chose?	4) T:	Did you buy anything?
5) S:	Ma grand-mère a acheté *du laine* pour faire euh euh…tu sais…	5) S:	My grandmother bought wool (masc.) to make, um, you know…
6) T:	*Du laine *	6) T:	Wool (masc.)?
7) S:	De la laine.	7) S:	Wool (fem.).
8) T:	Pour faire quoi?	8) T:	To make what?
9) S:	Uhm, tu sais des dessins là…	9) S:	Um, you know those drawings…

In response to the student's non-target *j'ai allé*, Rachelle provides a metalinguistic clue in line 2 that includes a repetition of the error: *J'ai allé, ça ne se dit pas*. This incites the student to self-repair in line 3 and then continue his story about going to the mall. Rachelle then repeats the student's non-target *du laine*, which incites him to self-repair in line 7 and then continue his story in line 9.

In Example 6, also from Rachelle's fourth-grade classroom, a student describes a ski trip with friends and family.

Example 8.6

1) S:	Puis là elle est allée avec ses parents et puis on a fait du ski ensemble. Puis là moi *j'ai revenu* euh vendredi…	1) S:	And so she went with her parents and then we skied together. And so I *camed* back uhm Friday…
2) T:	*J'ai revenu?*	2) T:	I *camed* back?
3) S:	Je suis revenue vendredi faire des [?]	3) S:	I came back Friday to do some [?]
4) T:	Très bien. Tu, tu es demeurée au Mont Ste-Anne toute la semaine?	4) T:	Very good. Did you stay at Mont Ste-Anne all week?

Rachelle again draws attention to a student's non-target utterance by repeating it in line 2 (*j'ai revenu*), in a way that succeeds in getting the student to self-repair in line 3 (*Je suis revenue*) and continue her story. Important to note is that students are in control of the content in these exchanges, as they relate what they did during their vacation, unlike Marie's lesson about the water cycle, where students were presented complex subject matter. Although most feasible in contexts where students are familiar with the content, prompts are not restricted to conversations about weekend and holiday activities. Exchanges described in Lyster (2002) show Rachelle prompting her students in similar ways during a science lesson about various mammals' means of defense, a topic with which students were already familiar.

The prompts in these examples do not damage conversational coherence and so the conversation continues, thus countering claims made by Krashen (1994) and Truscott (1999) that oral feedback causes anxiety, breaks the communicative flow, and remains difficult for teachers to provide and for students to notice. Moreover, in Lyster and Mori's (2006) comparison of French and Japanese immersion classrooms, whereas we found that recasts were much more effective in one setting than the other, prompts proved to be equally effective in both instructional settings, with learner uptake following 88% of all prompts in French immersion classrooms and 89% of all prompts in Japanese immersion classrooms. However, the important question is, of course, not whether students are able to modify or enhance their output immediately following prompts, but whether or not this type of feedback has more lasting effects. Whereas some studies have shown recasts to be more effective than no feedback at all when provided consistently during one-on-one interaction (e.g., Long, Inagaki, & Ortega, 1998; Mackey & Philp, 1998), recent classroom studies have shown that, in comparison to recasts, prompts are more effective, in both the short- and long-term. This was demonstrated for the acquisition of possessive determiners in English (Ammar, 2003) and also grammatical gender in French (Lyster, 2004). Moreover, Ammar (2003) found that prompts were particularly effective for low-proficiency learners whereas high-proficiency learners, arguably because their language-analytic abilities enabled them to notice recasts, benefited equally from prompts and recasts. Arguably, the effectiveness of prompts is related to the opportunities for meaningful practice they create, which enable learners to retrieve newly acquired forms during online production. As de Bot (1996) argued, second language learners benefit more from being pushed to retrieve target language forms than from merely hearing the forms in the input, because the retrieval and subsequent production stimulate the development of connections in memory. This argument finds support in the results of experimental research on the "generation effect" whereby learners remember information better when they take an active part in producing it, rather than having it provided by an external source (e.g., deWinstanley & Bjork, 2004).

Conclusion

The need for learners to notice target features in input, in order to process them as intake, is a crucial first step in second language acquisition (Schmidt, 1990). Positive input enhancement provides an effective tool for triggering such noticing. While positive input enhancement can be effectively employed to induce noticing, it is best supported by follow-up elaboration that includes rule-discovery tasks or metalinguistic explanation. Moreover, such noticing and awareness activities are likely to be most successful in conjunction with opportunities for practice and also feedback (Ranta & Lyster, 2006). In other words, positive input enhancement on its own does not constitute a sufficient pedagogical intervention. Its effectiveness is commensurate with the quality of complementary activities designed specifically to consolidate and reinforce the new knowledge gained from deliberately enhanced input.

Similarly, negative input enhancement, especially in the form of recasts, has proven effective in some classroom settings more than others, with effectiveness increasing in classrooms whose communicative orientation is relatively form-focused. Prompts have generally proven more effective across a wider range of classroom settings (from form-focused to meaning-focused) and for a wider range of learners (both low- and high-proficiency learners). This suggests, again, that negative input enhancement in the form of recasting provides one possible feedback type but needs to be used in tandem with other feedback types that push learners toward output enhancement.

Claims about the effectiveness of one type of feedback over another arguably reflect specific theoretical orientations. Recasts fit well with claims that negotiated interaction promotes second language development by providing opportunities for learners to notice the gap between interlanguage and target-like forms (e.g., Doughty, 2001; Long, 1996). Prompts fit well with skill acquisition theory (DeKeyser, 1998, 2001), given their pedagogical aim to provide opportunities to practice and thereby proceduralize recently acquired forms. Perhaps a more constructive perspective would be that the rationale for using these different types of feedback does not derive from theoretically incompatible views at all, and is instead reconciled in the view that there are two types of acquisition: acquisition as the internalization of new forms and acquisition as an increase in control over forms that have already been internalized (Bialystok & Sharwood Smith, 1985;

de Bot, 1996; Ellis, 1997; Nobuyoshi & Ellis, 1993; Takashima & Ellis, 1999). In this view, recasts serve as exemplars of positive evidence (Braidi, 2002; Leeman, 2003) and, in discourse contexts where they cannot be perceived ambiguously as approving the use of non-target forms, can be expected to facilitate the encoding of new target representations in declarative knowledge. Prompts, given their aim to elicit modified output, can enhance control over already-internalized forms, thereby assisting learners in the transition of declarative to procedural knowledge. Both types of acquisition are arguably of equal importance in second language classrooms. Enhancing classroom input, therefore, is but one important component of effective second language pedagogy; prompting learners to enhance their output is yet another.

Questions and Topics for Discussion

1) In Day and Shapson's (1991) study of the effects of instruction on the acquisition of the conditional in French, students were asked to play the role of ecologists and to design a space station that would recreate a natural environment where space pioneers would be able to settle. The objective was to provide students with a context for using the conditional to express possible yet uncertain outcomes in the future. However, the researchers reported having observed a tendency during the oral tasks for students to avoid the conditional and instead to use the present tense as they interacted together in groups. Test results indeed showed that progress made by students was more significant in writing than in speaking. What solutions can you propose that would encourage students to use required target forms during oral collaborative tasks?

2) In their comparison of French and Japanese immersion programs, Lyster and Mori (2006) found that the overall communicative orientation in Japanese immersion classrooms was more form-focused than French immersion classrooms insofar as students occasionally were engaged in choral repetition and practice activities emphasizing speaking as an isolated skill. What other factors might be at play that make Japanese immersion classrooms more form-focused than French immersion classrooms?

3) This chapter mentions many different types of corrective feedback techniques that teachers have at their disposal. What are some other feedback types that were not mentioned?

Notes

1) The following conventions are used in the extracts: T = teacher; S = student; Ss = more than one student; S1, S2, etc. = a student different from the speaker in the previous student turn. Relevant errors are bracketed by asterisks.

References

Ammar, A. (2003). *Corrective feedback and L2 learning: Elicitation and recasts.* Unpublished doctoral dissertation, McGill University, Montreal.

Bialystok, E., & Sharwood Smith, M. (1985). Interlanguage is not a state of mind. *Applied Linguistics, 6,* 101-117.

Braidi, S. (2002). Reexamining the role of recasts in native-speaker/nonnative-speaker interactions. *Language Learning, 52,* 1-42.

Day, E., & Shapson, S. (1991). Integrating formal and functional approaches to language teaching in French immersion: An experimental study. *Language Learning, 41,* 25-58.

de Bot, K. (1996). The psycholinguistics of the output hypothesis. *Language Learning, 46,* 529-555.

de Bot, K. (2000). Psycholinguistics in applied linguistics: Trends and perspectives. *Annual Review of Applied Linguistics, 20,* 224-237.

DeKeyser, R. (1998). Beyond focus on form: Cognitive perspectives on learning and practicing second language grammar. In C. Doughty & J. Williams (Eds.), *Focus on form in classroom second language acquisition* (pp. 42-63). Cambridge: Cambridge University Press.

DeKeyser, R. (2001). Automaticity and automatization. In P. Robinson (Ed.), *Cognition and second language instruction* (pp. 125-151). Cambridge: Cambridge University Press.

deWinstanley, P., & Bjork, E. (2004). Processing strategies and the generation effect: Implications for making a better reader. *Memory & Cognition, 32,* 945-955.

Doughty, C. (1994). Finetuning of feedback by competent speakers to language learners. In J. Alatis (Ed.), *GURT 1993: Strategic interaction* (pp. 96-108). Washington, DC: Georgetown University Press.

Doughty, C. (2001). Cognitive underpinnings of focus on form. In P. Robinson (Ed.), *Cognition and second language instruction* (pp. 206-257). Cambridge: Cambridge University Press.

Doughty, C., & Varela, E. (1998). Communicative focus on form. In C. Doughty & J. Williams (Eds.), *Focus on form in classroom second language acquisition* (pp. 129-154). Cambridge: Cambridge University Press.

Doughty, C., & Williams, J. (1998). Pedagogical choices in focus on form. In C. Doughty & J. Williams (Eds.), *Focus on form in classroom second language acquisition* (pp. 197-262). Cambridge: Cambridge University Press.

Ellis, R. (1997). *SLA research and language teaching*. Oxford: Oxford University Press.

Ellis, R. (2001). Investigating form-focused instruction. *Language Learning, 51* (Suppl. 1), 1-46.

Ellis, R., Basturkmen, H., & Loewen, S. (2001). Learner uptake in communicative ESL lessons. *Language Learning, 51,* 281-318.

Gass, S. (1997). *Input, interaction, and the second language learner*. Mahwah, NJ: Lawrence Erlbaum.

Genesee, F. (1987). *Learning through two languages: Studies of immersion and bilingual children*. Cambridge, MA: Newbury House.

Genesee, F. (1991). Second language learning in school settings: Lessons from immersion. In A. Reynolds (Ed.), *Bilingualism, multiculturalism, and second language learning* (pp. 183-202). Hillsdale, NJ: Lawrence Erlbaum.

Harley, B. (1989). Functional grammar in French immersion: A classroom experiment. *Applied Linguistics, 10,* 331-359.

Harley, B. (1993). Instructional strategies and SLA in early French immersion. *Studies in Second Language Acquisition, 15,* 245-259.

Harley, B. (1998). The role of form-focused tasks in promoting child L2 acquisition. In C. Doughty & J. Williams (Eds.), *Focus on form in classroom second language acquisition* (pp. 156-174). Cambridge: Cambridge University Press.

Harley, B., Allen P., Cummins, J., & Swain, M. (Eds.). (1990). *The development of second language proficiency*. Cambridge: Cambridge University Press.

Harley, B., Cummins, J., Swain, M., & Allen, P. (1990). The nature of language proficiency. In B. Harley, P. Allen, J. Cummins & M. Swain (Eds.), *The development of second language proficiency* (pp. 7-25). Cambridge: Cambridge University Press.

Lambert, W., & Tucker, R. (1972). *Bilingual education of children: The St. Lambert experiment*. Rowley, MA: Newbury House.

Lapkin, S., & Swain, M. (1996). Vocabulary teaching in a grade 8 French immersion classroom: A descriptive study. *The Canadian Modern Language Review, 53,* 242-256.

Laplante, B. (1993). Stratégies pédagogiques et enseignement des sciences en immersion française: Le cas d'une enseignante. *The Canadian Modern Language Review, 49,* 567-588.

Leeman, J. (2003). Recasts and second language development: Beyond negative evidence. *Studies in Second Language Acquisition, 25,* 37-63.

Krashen, S. (1994). The input hypothesis and its rivals. In N. Ellis (Ed.), *Implicit and explicit learning of languages* (pp. 45-77). London: Academic Press.

Lightbown, P. (1991). What have we here? Some observations on the influence of instruction on L2 learning. In R. Phillipson, E. Kellerman, L. Selinker, M. Sharwood Smith & M. Swain (Eds.), *Foreign/second language pedagogy research* (pp. 197-212). Clevedon, UK: Multilingual Matters.

Lightbown, P. (1998). The importance of timing in focus on form. In C. Doughty & J. Williams (Eds.), *Focus on form in classroom second language acquisition* (pp. 177-196). Cambridge: Cambridge University Press.

Long, M. (1991). Focus on form: A design feature in language teaching methodology. In K. de Bot, R. Ginsberg, & C. Kramsch (Eds.), *Foreign language research in cross-cultural perspective* (pp. 39-52). Amsterdam: Benjamins.

Long, M. (1996). The role of the linguistic environment in second language acquisition. In W. C. Ritchie & T. K. Bhatia (Eds.), *Handbook of second language acquisition* (pp. 413-468). San Diego, CA: Academic Press.

Long, M.H., Inagaki, S., & Ortega, L. (1998). The role of implicit negative feedback in SLA: Models and recasts in Japanese and Spanish. *Modern Language Journal, 82*, 357-371.

Long, M., & Robinson, P. (1998). Focus on form: Theory, research, and practice. In C. Doughty & J. Williams (Eds.), *Focus on form in classroom second language acquisition* (pp. 15-41). Cambridge: Cambridge University Press.

Lyster, R. (1994a). The effect of functional-analytic teaching on aspects of French immersion students' sociolinguistic competence. *Applied Linguistics, 15,* 263-287.

Lyster, R. (1994b). La négociation de la forme: Stratégie analytique en classe d'immersion. *The Canadian Modern Language Review, 50,* 446-465.

Lyster, R. (1998a). Recasts, repetition, and ambiguity in L2 classroom discourse. *Studies in Second Language Acquisition, 20*, 55-85.

Lyster, R. (1998b). Immersion pedagogy and implications for language teaching. In J. Cenoz & F. Genesee (Eds.), *Beyond bilingualism: Multilingualism and multilingual education* (pp. 64-95). Clevedon, UK: Multilingual Matters.

Lyster, R. (2002). Negotiation in immersion teacher-student interaction. *International Journal of Educational Research, 37*, 237-253.

Lyster, R. (2004). Differential effects of prompts and recasts in form-focused instruction. *Studies in Second Language Acquisition, 26*, 399-432.

Lyster, R., & Mori, H. (2006). Interactional feedback and instructional counterbalance. *Studies in Second Language Acquisition, 28*, in press.

Lyster, R., & Ranta, L. (1997). Corrective feedback and learner uptake: Negotiation of form in communicative classrooms. *Studies in Second Language Acquisition, 19,* 37-66.

Mackey, A., & Philp, J. (1998). Conversational interaction and second language development: Recasts, responses, and red herrings? *Modern Language Journal, 82,* 338-356.

Mori, H. (2002). *Error treatment sequences in Japanese immersion classroom interactions at different grade levels.* Unpublished doctoral dissertation, University of California, Los Angeles.

Nicholas, H., Lightbown, P., & Spada, N. (2001). Recasts as feedback to language learners. *Language Learning, 51,* 719-758.

Nobuyoshi, J., & Ellis, R. (1993). Focused communication tasks and second language acquisition. *ELT Journal, 47,* 203-210.

Panova, I., & Lyster, R. (2002). Patterns of corrective feedback and uptake in an adult ESL classroom. *TESOL Quarterly, 36,* 573-595.

Pica, T. (1994). Research on negotiation: What does it reveal about second-language learning conditions, processes, and outcomes? *Language Learning, 44,* 493-527.

Pica, T., Lincoln-Porter, F., Paninos, D., & Linnell, J. (1996). Language learners' interaction: How does it address the input, output, and feedback needs of language learners? *TESOL Quarterly, 30,* 59-84.

Ranta, L., & Lyster, R. (2006). A cognitive approach to improving immersion students' oral language abilities: The Awareness-Practice-Feedback sequence. In R. DeKeyser (Ed.), *Practicing for second language use: Perspectives from applied linguistics and cognitive psychology* (in press). Cambridge: Cambridge University Press.

Rebuffot, J., & Lyster, R. (1996). L'immersion au Canada: Contextes, effets et pédagogie. In J. Erfurt (Ed.), *De la polyphonie à la symphonie. Méthodes, théories et faits de la recherche pluridisciplinaire sur le français au Canada* (pp. 277-294). Leipzig: Leipziger Universitätsverlag GmbH.

Roberts, M. (1995). Awareness and the efficacy of error correction. In R. Schmidt (Ed.), *Attention and awareness in foreign language learning* (Tech. Rep. No. 9) (pp.162-182). Honolulu: University of Hawai'i.

Schmidt, R. (1990). The role of consciousness in second language learning. *Applied Linguistics, 11,* 129-158.

Sharwood Smith, M. (1981). Consciousness-raising and the second language learner. *Applied Linguistics, 2,* 159-168.

Sharwood Smith, M. (1993). Input enhancement in instructed SLA. *Studies in Second Language Acquisition, 15,* 165-179.

Sheen, Y. (2004). Corrective feedback and learner uptake in communicative classrooms across instructional settings. *Language Teaching Research, 8,* 263-300.

Spada, N. (1997). Form-focused instruction and second language acquisition: A review of classroom and laboratory research. *Language Teaching, 29,* 1-15.

Spada, N., & Fröhlich, M. (1995). *COLT. Communicative Orientation of Language Teaching observation scheme: Coding conventions and applications*. Sydney, Australia: National Centre for English Language Teaching and Research.

Swain, M. (1985). Communicative competence: Some roles of comprehensible input and comprehensible output in its development. In S. Gass & C. Madden (Eds.), *Input in second language acquisition* (pp. 235-253). Rowley, MS: Newbury House.

Swain, M. (1988). Manipulating and complementing content teaching to maximize second language learning. *TESL Canada Journal, 6*, 68-83.

Swain, M. (1996). Integrating language and content in immersion classrooms: Research perspectives. *The Canadian Modern Language Review, 52*, 529-548.

Takashima, H., & Ellis, R. (1999). Output enhancement and the acquisition of the past tense. In R. Ellis (Ed.), *Learning a second language through interaction* (pp. 173-188). Amsterdam/Philadelphia: John Benjamins.

Tomasello, M., & Herron, C. (1988). Down the garden path: Inducing and correcting overgeneralization errors in the foreign language classroom. *Applied Psycholinguistics, 9*, 237-246.

Tomasello, M., & Herron, C. (1989). Feedback for language transfer errors: The garden path technique. *Studies in Second Language Acquisition, 11*, 385-395.

Truscott, J. (1999). What's wrong with oral grammar correction. *The Canadian Modern Language Review, 55*, 437-456.

Tsang, W. (2004). Feedback and uptake in teacher-student interaction: An analysis of 18 English lessons in Hong Kong secondary classrooms. *Regional Language Centre Journal, 35*, 187-209.

VanPatten, B. (1990). Attending to form and content in the input: An experiment in consciousness. Studies in Second Language Acquisition, 12, 287-301.

White, J. (1998). Getting the learners' attention: A typographical input enhancement study. In C. Doughty & J. Williams (Eds.), *Focus on form in classroom second language acquisition* (pp. 85-113). Cambridge: Cambridge University Press.

Chapter 9
Input Enhancement by Natural Language Processing
Noriko Nagata, University of San Francisco

This chapter focuses on consciousness-raising input enhancement by computer. Input enhancement is interpreted as a pedagogical means that makes specific items of input more salient and draws learners' attention to those items (Sharwood Smith, 1993). Similarly, consciousness-raising is defined as the salience of underlying grammatical structures (Nagata & Swisher, 1995; Rutherford, 1987; Rutherford & Sharwood Smith, 1985). (See also Polio, this volume for a detailed discussion of the evolving use of these terms.) Consciousness-raising activities vary from explicit explanations of applicable grammatical rules to mere presentation of examples relevant to problematic constructions (Doughty, 1991).

It is, therefore, an interesting pedagogical question to determine which sorts of consciousness-raising activities to associate with different language learning tasks. Sharwood Smith (1993), for example, suggests that teaching meta-linguistic rules is such an elaborate form of input enhancement that the time spent training the learner in the appropriate concepts and terms should be justified by a corresponding facilitation in learning.

I have conducted a series of empirical studies, based on computer programs I developed, to investigate the effectiveness of different types of feedback to student attempts at producing language. The types of feedback considered include explicit explanation of grammatical rules, presentation of relevant examples, error messages concerning wrong or missing words, and first language translation of target patterns. I have also studied the effectiveness of different kinds of tasks including comprehension-based practice, production-based practice, and multiple-choice exercises. The next sections present some of the empirical studies and draw upon pedagogical morals for computer-assisted language education.

The type of task presented to the student and the kind of feedback provided by educational software depend upon whether or not the software incorporates natural language processing technology. **Natural Language Processing** (NLP) is an artificial intelligence technique that parses or decomposes linguistic input according to the grammatical rules and lexicon of the target language and determines whether the input sentence is grammatical or not. The results of the parse can be used to generate detailed feedback to explain grammatical principles violated in the learner's sentence. Therefore, this technology makes possible extensive sentence-level production exercises in which the learner can produce any sentence in response to an exercise and can receive grammatical feedback pinpointed to the precise nature of his or her errors. This type of feedback is called **intelligent feedback**. Conventional computer programs do not have natural language processing technology, so sentence analysis is limited to simple character-by-character matching of the learner's input to the machine-stored correct version. This is why tasks provided by conventional programs tend to be mostly fill-in-the-blank or multiple-choice exercises that do not involve sentence-level analysis. Feedback is also restricted to a small range of anticipated errors, indicating only which part is not matched with the correct answer, without any grammatical explanation of what is wrong. Such feedback is referred to as **traditional feedback** (Nagata, 1993).

I have developed a computer software package, *ROBO-SENSEI: Japanese Personal Tutor* (Nagata, 2004) (*sensei* means teacher) that employs natural language processing technology and provides extensive sentence production tasks together with intelligent feedback. I now proceed to the studies themselves.

Empirical Studies

The subjects who participated in the following experiments were all university students in beginning- or intermediate-level Japanese courses. Each experimental study involved two treatment groups created by a pairing system. That is, the student who obtained the highest score and the student who obtained the second highest score on a pretest were paired and were randomly assigned to either one of the two groups, until the last two students (the students with the two lowest scores) were randomly assigned to either group. Consequently, the two groups had no significant difference in the level of achievement in the course prior to treatment. The following discussion briefly summarizes the findings of the studies. Detailed descriptions of each study below are provided in Nagata, 1993, 1995, 1997a, 1997b, 1998a, 1998b, and 2002.

Intelligent Feedback versus Traditional Feedback

Nagata (1993) compared the relative effectiveness of intelligent feedback with traditional feedback. The study used Nihongo-CALI (Japanese Computer Assisted Language Instruction) which employed natural language processing. The students were asked to produce passive sentences based upon described situations. The traditional feedback group received traditional feedback messages of the sort typically provided by ordinary computer programs without natural language processing technology. The intelligent feedback group received intelligent feedback that can only be provided by means of natural language processing technology. For example, the following illustrates one of the exercises involving the Japanese "adversative-passive" construction (lit. "someone is adversely affected by someone else's action") together with the corresponding feedback.

Example 1

At a party your friend has asked if there are still Japanese drinks (left). Respond that no, the students went and drank all the Japanese beer (i.e, you were affected by the students' drinking all the Japanese beer).

Friend: *Nihon no nomimono ga mada aru?*
Your reponse:

A Japanese sentence, *Nihon no nomimono ga mada aru?* "Are there still Japanese drinks left?" was provided. A correct reponse for this question is *Uun, gakusee ni nihon no biiru o zenbu nomareta yo.* "No, I was affected by the students' drinking all the Japanese beer." Suppose the learner typed *Uun, gakusee ga nihon no biiru o zenbu nomaremasu.* "No, the students will be affected by someone's drinking all the Japanese beer." The error messages were provided as follows:

Traditional feedback:
- GA is not expected to be used here.
- NI is missing.
- NOMAREMASU is wrong.

Intelligent feedback:
- GA is not expected to be used here.
- NI is missing.
- In your sentence, GAKUSEE is the 'subject' of the passive (the one that is affected by the action), but it should be the 'agent' of the passive (the one who performs the action and affects the subject). Use the particle NI to mark it.
- The predicate you typed is in the imperfective form. Change it to perfective. Since you are talking with your friend and your friend is using the direct-style (casual style), use the direct-style for your response.

In short, traditional feedback pinpoints which word is unexpected, missing, or wrong, but does not explain why. Intelligent feedback explains the grammatical rules involved in particle usage and verbal conjugations. (In Japanese, particles mark a grammatical or semantic function of each noun such as the subject, object, goal, location, and so forth.) In terms of consciousness-raising input enhancement, both traditional and intelligent feedback made the learners' erroneous words salient, but intelligent feedback drew the learners' attention explicitly to the grammatical rules related to the problematic areas.

The posttest showed a significant difference between the two groups, favoring the intelligent feedback group ($t=2.18$, $p<0.05$). The result confirms the effectiveness of enhancing feedback messages by explaining the nature of the students' errors in terms of grammatical rules.

The difference between the two groups was mostly attributable to particle errors. Other types of errors, such as vocabulary and verbal conjugation errors did not show a significant difference. Vocabulary and verbal conjugation errors are word-level errors, while particle errors are more complex, sentence-level errors. In Japanese, verbal conjugations do not involve agreement in number, gender, and so forth. Consequently, the production of verbal conjugations can be focused on the verb itself, without thinking of the nature of the subject and object in a sentence. On the other hand, assigning an appropriate particle to each noun phrase requires some understanding of grammatical relations between different noun phrases in a sentence, so syntactic processing is required.

Before beginning the computer sessions, the students in both groups received the same grammatical instruction about passive structures (i.e., the grammatical rules governing verbal conjugations and particle usage in passive sentences). The distribution of errors indicated that, given the initial explicit grammatical instruction, simple indication of word-level mistakes may suffice to correct word-level errors. On the other hand, ongoing, repeated, principle-based input enhancement is required to solve sentence-level errors such as particle errors. It would be interesting to further investigate the effectiveness of principle-based feedback with relation to different levels of errors and different complexities of target structures.

Intelligent Feedback versus Enhanced Traditional Feedback

The second experiment (Nagata, 1995) compared intelligent feedback with enhanced traditional feedback, which indicates not only missing particles but also their locations (e.g., when the student missed the particle *de*, the student was informed not only that "DE is missing," but also that "DE should be attached to KOOEN"). This level of feedback can be provided without natural language processing technology. The intelligent feedback, however, included rule-based grammatical explanations for the errors as in the previous study. The target grammar was beginning-level Japanese sentence construction using the basic particles, *wa, ga, o, ni,* and *de*.

The posttest results were consistent with the previous study, favoring the intelligent feedback group ($t=3.04$, $p<0.02$). The results indicate that additional information on the locations of missing particles is still not as effective as explicit rule explanations.

Metalinguistic versus English-Translation Feedback

Since particle acquisition is one of the major obstacles for learners of Japanese, Nagata (1997a) first investigated the strategies learners use to assign a particle in a sentence. An initial particle test was administered in which students were asked to fill in 32 blanks with appropriate particles and to explain why those particles were used. The students were in a fourth-semester Japanese course, and a variety of relatively complex particles introduced up to the intermediate level were included in this study. The results suggest that the students employed two main strategies to assign a particle in a sentence: (1) following metalinguistic rules (MR) and (2) relying on English L1 (first language) translations (ET). For example, for the explanation of the particle *de* in the sentence *Nihon de nani o kenkyuu-saremasita ka* "What did you research in Japan?" one of the MRs was "use DE for place of action" and one of the ETs was "in Japan." Group 1 obtained a total of 155 correct particles in which 76 correct particles were accompanied by correctly applied metalinguistic rules (MR), 45 correct particles were followed by correct English translations (ET), and 34 correct particles were given incorrect/incomplete explanations (I). Similarly, Group 2 obtained a total of 164 correct particles, in which 88 correct particles were explained correctly by MRs, 52 correct particles were followed by correct ETs, and 24 correct particles were in the (I) category.

Based on these two strategies, two types of feedback were implemented in the computer program in response to the students' particle errors: one group received metalinguistic feedback (i.e., detailed explanations about grammatical and semantic functions of the particles, which were the equivalent to the intelligent feedback used in the previous studies) and the other group received ET feedback (i.e., English L1 translations of Japanese particles) rather than MR-assigned case roles.

The result was that the metalinguistic feedback group performed significantly better on an achievement test than the translation feedback group ($t=2.69$, $p<0.02$). Group 1 showed a much stronger tendency to use metalinguistic rules than Group 2 when arriving at correct particles on the achievement test. The results indicate that metalinguistic feedback led the Group 1 students to use a metalinguistic strategy more than English translation and that the English-translation feedback encouraged the Group 2 students to rely more on first-language translations than on metalinguistic rules. It appears that the English-translation feedback is too specific and did not help the Group 1 students to develop general competence in the use of particles. The results suggest that consciousness-raising metalinguistic feedback reinforces the learner's metalinguistic ability and leads to better performance in the production of complex grammatical structures than does merely providing first-language translations.

Deductive Feedback versus Inductive Feedback

Nagata (1997b) investigated the relative effectiveness of teaching explicit grammatical rules as opposed to providing relevant examples without rule instruction, which has been a subject of continuing debate in SLA research (DeKeyser, 1995). This debate also raises an important design question for computer feedback. Accordingly, two types of feedback were implemented into an earlier version of ROBO-SENSEI, called the BANZAI Particle Tutor, which already incorporated natural language processing technology. This program was designed to provide practice on the Japanese basic particles (*wa, ga, o, ni,* and *de*) and sentence constructions.

The following illustrates one of the exercises provided by the BANZAI Particle Tutor.

Example 2

Your tutor has just asked what you did last night. Respond that you wrote a letter to a friend in Japanese.

A correct answer is *Tomodati ni nihongo de tegami o kakimasita*, "I wrote a letter to a friend in Japanese." Suppose a student types the sentence *Tegami wa tomodati ga nihongo kakimasita*, which includes several particle errors. The following illustrates the deductive and inductive feedback for this response.

- A particle is missing for NIHONGO. It should be marked with the particle DE to indicate the role INSTRUMENT (the one by means of which the action occurs).
- You used the particle GA to mark TOMODATI as though it had the role SUBJECT (the one who performs the action). But the correct role is GOAL (the goal of the action). Use NI to mark it.
- You used the particle WA to mark TEGAMI as though it had the role TOPIC or CONTRAST. But TEGAMI was not under discussion before. Use O to mark the role OBJECT (the one that the action operated upon).

Inductive feedback

- A particle is missing for NIHONGO. It should be marked with the particle DE. The following examples show how the particle DE is used.
  1) *Waapuro de kakimasita.* "I wrote it with a word processor."
  2) *Basu de ikimasita.* "I went by bus."
- You used the particle GA to mark TOMODATI, but the correct particle is NI. The following examples show how the particles NI and GA are used.

Particle NI: 1) *Tanaka-san ni kakimasu.* "I will write to Mr./Ms. Tanaka."
2) *Tomodati ni misemasu.* "I will show it to my friend."

Particle GA: 1) *Tanaka-san ga ikimasu.* "Mr./Ms. Tanaka will go."
2) *Tomodati ga tukurimasita.* "My friend made it."

- You used the particle WA to mark TEGAMI, but the correct particle is O. The following examples show how the particles O and WA are used.

Particle O: 1) *Susi o tukurimasita.* "I made sushi."
2) *Nani o tabemasita ka.* "What did you eat?"

Particle WA: 1) (talking about Ms. Smith)
Sumisu-san wa keeki o tukurimasita. "As for Ms. Smith, she made cake."
2) (talking about the kanji)
Sono kanzi wa watasi ga kakimasita. "As for that kanji, I wrote it."
3) (talking about pie and ice cream)
Pai wa tabemasen desita. "I didn't eat any pie (but ate some ice cream)."

The inductive version of the BANZAI program stored two or three sample sentences per particle that are presented to the student whenever he or she commits an error related to the particle in question. As is apparent in the above examples, the screen soon becomes cluttered if more than a few examples are provided for each particle. Accordingly, two example sentences per particle were presented (three for the particle *wa*). Whether or not more examples (or different kinds of examples) would yield better results is an interesting question for future study.

A significant difference was found between the two groups, favoring the deductive group in the posttest (t=4.04, p<0.002 for the fill-in-the-blank tasks and t=3.55, p<0.005 for the sentence-production tasks), in the retention test (a month later) (t=4.94, p<0.005 for the fill-in-the-blank tasks and t=3.39, p<0.005 for the sentence-production tasks), and in the oral conversation test (five weeks later) (t=3.19, p<0.01).

The above tests exclusively involved production-based tasks as the students practiced on the computer. In addition, students were given immediate and delayed comprehension tests in which they were asked to translate Japanese conversations into English. The sentences used in the comprehension tests were also similar to those provided by the computer exercises. Neither of the comprehension tests showed a significant difference between the deductive group and the inductive group. This may be explained by the fact that once the meaning of each word in a sentence is understood, it could be interpreted without relying on syntactic cues presented by the particles. This is consistent with Flynn's (1986) hypothesis that grammatical competence is less critical in comprehension than in production since other extralinguistic knowledge and information available to the subject can be used to make a coherent interpretation of the stimulus sentence (see also VanPatten, this volume and Wong, this volume).

The results indicate that the Japanese particle functions are not sufficiently salient given the examples, so the inductive feedback group, which merely observed the example sentences, could not develop a clear understanding of the particle functions in spite of the fact that they read the grammar note that explained the relevant metalinguistic rules before starting the exercises. On the other hand, the deductive feedback group received ongoing metalinguistic explanations in response to their errors and such feedback made the target principles salient and helped them to increase their understanding of the particle functions. The results support the importance of repeated deductive feedback to reinforce learners' grammatical knowledge as applied to the task of producing the target structures.

Comprehension Practice versus Production Practice with Complex Structures

The studies presented above employed only production-based practice, but of course there are various ways of practicing a foreign language. For example, learners can be engaged solely in comprehending what they hear and read without producing sentences on their own. Such practice is said to provide comprehensible input (Krashen, 1985). This approach assumes that if learners receive a sufficient amount of comprehensible input, they will naturally be able to produce the language. (See Polio, this volume for a critique.) To test this thesis, Nagata (1998a) performed an experiment concerning the relative effectiveness of comprehension and production practice on the acquisition of Japanese honorifics, which are fairly complicated structures. The comprehension group received explicit grammatical instruction and comprehension exercises. The production group received the same grammatical instruction together with production exercises. The comprehension program employed a multiple-choice question format of the sort commonly used in comprehension exercises. Specifically, the student was provided choices from which to select a correct interpretation. The production program involved the same sentences used in the comprehension program, but the student had to produce the sentence. The program used a Japanese word processor so that the students could type their responses in the Japanese writing system. No parsing technique was involved in this study, so the analysis of the students' responses was done by simple pattern matching, and error feedback was limited to missing words/particles and incorrect/incomplete verbal forms. In short, both the comprehension and the production programs provided the same exercise content with equivalent grammatical feedback responding to students' correct answers and anticipated errors. The Japanese pronunciation of the correct answers was provided as well.

The results of the achievement test showed no significant difference between the two groups on the comprehension tasks, while a difference between the two groups on the production tasks was statistically significant, favoring the production group ($t=5.67$, $p<0.002$). A significant difference was found on sentence-level and paragraph-level tasks, but not for phrase-level and listening exercises. Phrase-level production tasks asked the students to fill in the blank with a verbal predicate. This type of question involves production of a verb form only, whereas sentence-production tasks require full-sentence production. Therefore, sentence-production tasks involve more complex syntactic processing than phrase-level tasks. Paragraph-level tasks are also more complex than phrase-level tasks because they require the students to read a paragraph and revise verbs in the text with appropriate honorific forms when necessary. In this type of task, the learners need to understand discourse context and recover some unstated subjects and objects from context in order to determine the appropriate honorific forms. The results suggest that when more complex syntactic and discourse processing is involved in production tasks, it becomes more difficult for learners to apply their learning from comprehension exercises directly to the production tasks. In the listening production tasks, students were presented a few Japanese sentences orally and were asked to write them down, which is different from constructing sentences from scratch. In this task, an oral cue was provided three times for each sentence, and students were given enough time to write down each sentence. The fact that the nature of the task was half-receptive might be one reason why the comprehension group performed as well as the production group on listening production tasks.

The retention test results are consistent with the achievement test results: there is no significant difference between the two groups on the comprehension tasks, while the difference between the two groups on the production tasks is statistically significant, favoring the production group ($t=3.18$, $p<0.02$). The oral conversation task also exhibits a statistically significant difference, favoring the production group ($t=3.29$, $p<0.02$).

In sum, the results of the study suggest that given the same grammatical instruction, production practice is more effective than comprehension practice for the development of grammatical skill in producing Japanese honorifics and is equally effective for the comprehension of these structures. This is consistent with Swain's (1985) hypothesis that producing language, as opposed to simply comprehending it, can force the learner to move from semantic processing to syntactic processing, thereby improving grammatical performance (see also Swain & Lapkin, 1995). The analysis of different types of exercises suggests that the relative advantage of production practice may be greater in tasks involving complex syntactic processing than in tasks requiring less syntactic processing. The results also indicate that consciousness-raising activities are more effective through production practice than through comprehension practice in the acquisition of Japanese honorifics.

Comprehension Practice versus Production Practice with Simple Structures

The previous study employed Japanese honorifics, fairly complicated structures. A subsequent study (Nagata, 1998b) addressed the question of whether the advantage of production practice over comprehension practice is still obtained when the target structures are relatively simple. The target structures used in the study were nominal modifiers such as an adjective or noun modifying a preceding noun.

The results were consistent with those in the preceding study: there was no significant difference between the two groups on the comprehension scores, but a significant difference was found on the production scores, favoring the production group ($t=4.84$, $p<0.001$ in the posttest, $t=5.25$, $p<0.002$ on the retention test, and $t=2.25$, $p<0.05$ on the oral conversation test).

It was observed that Japanese nominal modifiers were interpretable without processing the syntactic cues *no* and *na*. For example, once learners understood that *tomodati* means "friend," *kuruma* "car," and *kiree* "pretty," it was easy to interpret *tomodati no kuruma* as "a friend's car" and *kiree na kuruma* as "a pretty car" without processing *no* and *na*. On the other hand, production required the correct use of such syntactic cues. Even though the structures were relatively simple (using either *no*, *na*, or none), comprehension practice alone was not sufficient to draw learners' attention to those forms. The results confirm that consciousness-raising grammatical instruction is more effective through production practice than through comprehension practice, since production practice draws more attention to syntactic patterns and leads to better performance in producing target sentences.

Production Exercises versus Multiple-Choice Exercises

As discussed earlier, ordinary computer programs provide mostly multiple-choice or fill-in-the-blank exercises because they lack natural language processing capability. ROBO-SENSEI, on the other hand, has natural language processing technology, so it can analyze the student's sentence and return detailed feedback. Another study (Nagata, 2002) compared ROBO-SENSEI's production exercises with conventional multiple-choice exercises. The production group was asked to produce a sentence based on the situation provided. The multiple-choice group was provided the same exercise content, but was asked to choose a correct sentence from six sentences, five of which contained various errors. The study employed ROBO-SENSEI's Module 2 (Particle Lessons) for students in first-semester Japanese, and Module 7 (Relative Clause Lessons) for students in third-semester Japanese. The multiple-choice exercises included possible responses involving errors in target particles, vocabulary, and predicate forms. Both groups received intelligent feedback in response to their errors because ROBO-SENSEI's natural language processing engine was used for both types of exercises, so in this sense the multiple-choice program used in the study provided more flexible, detailed feedback than ordinary computer programs can manage.

The posttest results from ROBO-SENSEI's Modele 2 (Particle Lessons) showed that the production group performed significantly better than the multiple-choice group on both production tasks (t=2.82, p<0.01) and multiple-choice tasks (t=2.58, p<0.05). I expected that the multiple-choice group would perform at least as well as the production group on the multiple-choice tasks. The posttest results from ROBO-SENSEI's Module 7 (Relative Clause Lessons) revealed that the production group performed significantly better than the multiple-choice group on the production tasks (t=2.85, p<0.01), and did as well as the multiple-choice group on the multiple-choice tasks (t=0.31). The results again suggest that consciousness-raising activities are more effective when provided with production tasks. That is, students in the production group paid more attention to the grammatical forms they needed for producing target sentences and developed better grammatical skills than the multiple-choice group. Consequently, even though the production group did not practice multiple-choice exercises, they could distinguish well-formed sentences from ill-formed sentences on the posttest multiple-choice tasks better than the multiple-choice group in both the Particle and the Relative Clause Modules.

Summary of the Empirical Results

The series of empirical studies in this chapter examined the effectiveness of consciousness-raising activities with different types of feedback and on different kinds of tasks. The results evidence the effectiveness of principle-based intelligent feedback (1) over traditional feedback that pinpoints missing/unexpected/wrong words but does not explain general grammatical rules involved in the errors, (2) over first-language translation feedback that presents an English translation of the correct phrase, and (3) over example-based feedback that provides example sentences that illustrate target structures. The results indicate that input enhancement with appropriate grammatical concepts and rules is more effective than input enhancement without explanations involving grammatical principles. The results also support the cognitive approach, which emphasizes principle-based grammatical instruction for language learning (Omaggio, 1986). The studies reveal the importance of immediate, repeated, individualized feedback, which is very limited in regular classroom instruction. Students need ongoing, detailed grammatical feedback in response to their errors to reinforce their understanding of underlying grammatical principles. Finally, production practice is essential for developing production skills and improving grammatical performance. Simply comprehending a sentence (comprehension practice) or choosing a correct sentence (multiple-choice practice) does not involve syntactic processing as deep as production tasks require, and learning from comprehension or multiple-choice exercises cannot be transferred easily to full sentence production, which is a necessary component of genuine mastery.

Questions and Topics for Discussion

1) Discuss why traditional, manual coding techniques are not feasible for analyzing sentences or providing detailed grammatical feedback via computer (think about how many possible correct responses there are for a given example and about how many different sorts of errors the program would have to address).
2) Discuss the conditions in which principle-based feedback is more effective than other types of feedback.
3) Discuss why comprehension practice itself is not sufficient and why production practice is required.
4) Based on the findings in this chapter, design a consciousness-raising activity and provide supporting arguments for the activity.

References

DeKeyser, R. (1995). Learning second language grammar rules: An experiment with a miniature linguistic system. *Studies in Second Language Acquisition, 17*, 379-410.

Doughty, C. (1991). Second language instruction does make a difference. *Studies in Second Language Acquisition, 13*, 431-469.

Flynn, S. (1986). Production versus comprehension: Differences in underlying competences. *Studies in Second Language Acquisition, 8*, 135-164.

Krashen, S. (1985). *The input hypothesis: Issues and implications*. London: Longman.

Nagata, N. (1993). Intelligent computer feedback for second language instruction. *The Modern Language Journal, 77*, 330-339.

Nagata, N. (1995). An effective application of natural language processing in second language instruction. *CALICO Journal, 13*, 47-67.

Nagata, N. (1997a). The effectiveness of computer-assisted metalinguistic instruction: A case study in Japanese. *Foreign Language Annals, 30*, 187-200.

Nagata, N. (1997b). An experimental comparison of deductive and inductive feedback generated by a simple parser. *System, 25*, 515-534.

Nagata, N. (1998a). Input versus output practice in educational software for second language acquisition. *Language Learning and Technology, 1*, 23-40.

Nagata, N. (1998b). The relative effectiveness of production and comprehension practice in second language acquisition. *Computer Assisted Language Learning, 11*, 153-177.

Nagata, N. (2002, November). *The BANZAI project: Empirical studies on the effectiveness of intelligent feedback and sentence production practice.* Paper presented at the American Council on the Teaching of Foreign Languages (ACTFL) Annual Meeting, Salt Lake City, UT.

Nagata, N. (2004). *ROBO-SENSEI: Personal Japanese tutor.* Boston: Cheng & Tsui.

Nagata, N., & Swisher, M. (1995). A study of consciousness-raising by computer: The effect of metalinguistic feedback on second language learning. *Foreign Language Annals, 28*, 337-347.

Omaggio, A. (1986). *Teaching language in context.* Boston: Heinle & Heinle.

Rutherford, W. (1987). *Second language grammar: Learning and teaching.* London: Longman.

Rutherford, W., & Sharwood Smith, M. (1985). Consciousness-raising and universal grammar. *Applied Linguistics, 6*, 274-282.

Sharwood Smith, M. (1993). Input enhancement in instructed SLA: Theoretical bases. *Studies in Second Language Acquisition,15*, 165-179.

Swain, M. (1985). Communicative competence: Some roles of comprehensible input and comprehensible output in its development. In S. Gass, & C. Madden (Eds.), *Input in second language acquisition* (pp. 235-253). Rowley, MA: Newbury House.

Swain, M., & Lapkin, S. (1995). Problems in output and the cognitive processes they generate: A step toward second language learning. *Applied Linguistics, 16*, 371-391.

Chapter 10
Some Thoughts on The Future of Research on Input Enhancement

Bill VanPatten, University of Illinois at Chicago

It is not surprising to see how the field of instructed SLA has moved over the years from the question of "Does instruction make a difference?" (e.g., Long, 1983) to the question that underlies the current volume: "In what ways, if at all, can we facilitate the process of language acquisition?" (cf., Doughty, 2003). With the acknowledgement that it is the data residing somewhere in the input that fuels language acquisition while at the same time learners possess internal mechanisms that interact with those data, the field has had to reassess just what instruction ought to be doing, could be doing, and why, if at all, it would have any impact on how learners interact with input. In a sense, we have finally come around to addressing S. Pit Corder's concern of almost 40 years ago:

> We have been reminded recently of von Humboldt's statement that we cannot really teach language, we can only create conditions in which it will develop spontaneously in the mind in its own way. We shall never improve our ability to create such favorable conditions until we learn more about the way a learner learns and what his built-in syllabus is. When we do know this...we may begin to be more critical of our cherished notions. (Corder, 1969, reprinted in Corder, 1981, pp. 12-13).

Because we have been steadfastly working at trying to understand acquisition as Corder urged us to, a number of once cherished notions have fallen away—at least in research circles. Here are several:

- Language acquisition is not habit formation.
- Practice—in any noncommunicative or nonmeaning-based sense, such as drill, repetition, fill-in-the-blank, and so on—does not make perfect.
- The first language is not the source of all problems in acquisition and indeed its influence may be constrained by certain universals of acquisition.
- Teaching structure X before structure Y does not mean that X will be acquired before Y.
- Learners do not acquire paradigms or sets of rules but rather connections of forms and lexical items as well as abstract rules that constrain what is possible in a given language.

We have come to understand that there is a lot more to acquisition tucked away inside the learner's mind-brain than we did 40 years ago (see, e.g., the collection in Doughty & Long, 2003; R. Ellis, 1994; Gass & Selinker, 2001). Thus, in the first decade of the 21st century we find the field of instructed SLA focusing on topics as diverse as text enhancement, processing instruction, pushed output, and others. Where are we headed with this collection of constructs? What are the driving research questions?

In this chapter, I would like to offer some thoughts on the future of research on input enhancement (IE). To do so, I would like to first summarize what I see as the substantial findings to date regarding IE. From that discussion, problem areas for research will emerge, areas that I believe need to be systematically addressed in the future. However, there is the sticky matter of what is meant by acquisition so I turn my attention to some definitions first.

What is Acquisition and What is Acquired?

Any research on SLA must include definitions of its constructs. As we examine the research on IE, two questions should immediately surface:
1) How does the researcher define acquisition?
2) What is it that exists in the acquired system?

These are not trivial questions, to be sure. For example, if a researcher studies the impact of IE on learners' acquisition of *avoir* and *être* for the passé composé in French, what does the researcher think the acquisition of this distinction is? What rule underlies their use? What exists in the learner's head in terms of this distinction? And how does the researcher measure whatever he or she thinks has happened? What kind of assessment is appropriate? In the research on IE to date, we tend to see pedagogical rules of grammar (as found in textbooks) most often being the foci of research. Does this mean the researcher believes the acquisition of language means the accumulation in the head of pedagogical rules? Does the brain really organize the difference between *être* and *avoir* in French when used with the passé composé in terms of the textbook rules given to students? If the researcher uses a paper and pencil test, what does the researcher believe he or she is tapping in order for the learner to take the test? And if the researcher uses some kind of oral measure with "spontaneous" data, what does the researcher believe he or she is assessing? (I will address the matter of assessment again in a later section.) In short, the definition of what acquisition is and what is acquired is critical to IE research and we can't be too cavalier about it.

For the purposes of the present discussion, I take acquisition to refer to how learners develop a mental representation of language, including all the formal properties (phonological, phonetic, morphological, syntactic) as well as functional (semantic, aspectual, pragmatic, and so on). By mental representation I mean that learners hold in their heads some kind of implicit and abstract linguistic system, implicit in that it exists outside of awareness (even though we may be aware we have it) and abstract in that what is contained in it is not the shorthand rules of textbooks or descriptive grammars (cf., L. White, 2003). Take for example what a learner of Spanish comes to know about the verb *poner*. Although a textbook may list this verb as "to put" which requires a theme and a destination in both English and Spanish, this correspondence breaks down when the verb is used reflexively. In English, "to put oneself" literally means to place one's self in a situation as in "I put myself in jeopardy." Such a meaning is true of Spanish as well (e.g., *Me puse en el medio* "I put myself in the middle") but the reflexive form is also used with adjectives to mean something quite different. *Se puso rojo como un tomate* means "He turned red like a tomato," meaning he was red from embarrassment (normally). The sense of a person doing something that places him or herself in a position or situation is gone. (There are other ways in which this verb differs from its English "counterpart" but this one example will be sufficient here to illustrate matters.) What the learner must do, then, is learn that the verb *poner* can combine with a reflexive pronoun to become an unaccusative. This requires abstract knowledge of both how unaccusatives work in Spanish (with and without reflexive pronouns) and which verbs can do this. This knowledge cannot be gleaned from the L1 necessarily as in the case of "put" and while the learner may be taught a handful of expressions and what they mean, it is his or her brain that organizes the information into abstract categories and features.

Let me give one more example with *poner*. One abstract property of the verb is animacy. Just as English requires an animate referent for the subject of "put" (Mary put the bun in the oven/The rock put the bun in the oven), so does *poner*, even when the verb is used in an intransitive manner. So, a person can *ponerse caliente* ("get heated," most often with a sexual connotation but not always); however, a pan on the stove *se calienta* ("gets warm"); the pan does not *ponerse caliente*. *Ponerse* is also used with the preposition *a* and an infinitive to mean to begin to do something as in *Se puso a llorar* ("He began to cry"). It is impossible to say **Se puso a llover* ("It began to rain"). The point here is that deeply embedded in the verb *poner* is the concept of animacy and no matter how the verb is used, animacy is manifested in either well-formedness and/or semantic acceptability. Learners "know this" and actually never make mistakes with *poner* when it does not translate as "to put."

It is important to note here that I am not defining acquisition as skill or as communicative language ability. Although important constructs for viewing the totality of second language acquisition and use, skill and communication are isolable from the development of a mental representation and the relationship between them and the representation seems to be clear: representation underlies skill and ability, not the other way around. Thus, the particular role of an interventionist technique must be circumscribed by what it purports to affect and in terms of IE the effects must be on the acquisition of the mental representation that underlies language use. Input enhancement is not a concept that can be related to productive skills and communication with language. Even though I have stated above that we can question what a researcher takes acquisition to be and that it may not be clear from the research study itself, I will assume the definition of acquisition in this section for the rest of this chapter.

Back to Input Enhancement: Where Are We So Far?

I take the following to be what we know about IE—in all of its manifestations from text enhancement to input flood to recasts to processing instruction and others. I cull from Wong (2005) for this list.

- IE has yielded conflicting findings. Sometimes it appears to be helpful, sometimes it doesn't.
- When IE appears to be helpful, it seems to be selective. Not all linguistic structures seem to benefit by IE and not all learners seem to respond equally to IE.
- Some types of IE seem to be (consistently) more effective than others.

This is not a particularly inviting set of findings for instructors, although for researchers it suggests that something is lurking in the bushes and needs to be flushed out. The major question that emerges when looking at this list is why IE is not more universally beneficial to learners. For example, research on text enhancement has yielded quite disparate findings. Researchers like Robinson (1995) find text enhancement to benefit learners. Researchers like Wong (2000) and J. White (1998) do not or get mixed results within the same study. It appears to me that there are two intervening variables that underlie the more general question of IE effectiveness and these are (1) the nature of the linguistic structure that is the target of acquisition and (2) the presence or absence of explicit information prior to treatment. In addition, explicit information as a variable invites discussion of research design more generally, given we must ask ourselves important questions about assessment measures (among other things). Finally, there is also the matter of long-term effects. I will take each of these issues in turn.

Type of Linguistic Structure

That the type of linguistic structure used in an instructional treatment might make a difference is not surprising; this notion has been around for some time in one way or another. It was around during the heyday of contrastive analysis, it was around in the heyday of monitor theory in Krashen's (1982 and elsewhere) comments on the effectiveness of explicit instruction for 'easy' rules, and it has been around in others' discussions about the more general effectives of any kind of instruction (see, e.g., Hulstijn, 1995, as well as deGraff, 1997). What is not at all clear is (1) why structure would make a difference and (2) how to categorize structures in some meaningful way acceptable to researchers and that would, in turn, yield research that could test the categories themselves.

The issue of linguistic structure chosen for research purposes is not trivial. The conclusions that a researcher arrives at regarding IE may very well be due to the linguistic structure selected for his or her study rather than to the overall effectiveness of IE. For example, research on attention and awareness has not paid systematic attention to the type of structure used in this line of research. Any conclusions about attention and awareness may thus be premature unless we know just how awareness and attention interact with particular linguistic structures or problems that particular structures present. It would be odd, indeed, to suggest that awareness is implicated in the acquisition of abstract properties of syntax or, say, certain kinds of allophonic variation. However, it makes perfect sense to suggest that awareness may be implicated in certain kinds of morphological properties of language (but not all) as well as the relationship between lexical forms and their meanings.

To date we have seen various factors used in categorizing ease/difficulty of linguistic structures:

- differences between L1 and L2;
- core versus peripheral features of the L2;
- abstract versus concrete rules (opaque versus transparent);
- simple versus complex structural properties.

As one example, consider deGraff's matrix for the selection of linguistic structures in his widely recognized study (deGraff, 1997). He selected structures based on whether they were morphological in nature (such as an inflection) or whether they were syntactic (such as position of something in a sentence). He then crossed this with whether the feature was simple (had no variation in form) or complex (had variation in form or in the case of syntactic features, had variation in terms of placement within a sentence). For his study on Spanish, he chose plural markers, imperative verb markers, the position of the simple negator, and object pronoun position.

As we examine these and similar categories an underlying assumption surfaces: *that structure is to be defined and categorized in terms of overt properties of the structure.* The use of such categories has, in my opinion, yielded some interesting findings but also some contradictory ones such as those in the deGraff study itself: complex does not always lead to more difficult and simple does not always lead to easier, although there are clear trends. In his study, deGraff found (among other things) that the effects of explicit instruction as part of IE depended more on the meaningfulness of the structure rather than its complexity: "when form-meaning connections are easily noticed [in the input], explicit instruction is less necessary for reaching accuracy; when the difference between forms is non-meaningful, the effect of explanation [again, as part of IE] is larger" (p. 151). Unfortunately, deGraff's focus was on the role of explicit information as part of IE and thus it is difficult to determine what might be the role of complexity. Nonetheless, his results suggest that even though there may be something to the notion of complexity, there are also other factors that may be just as important.

I believe there is an additional if not altogether different factor to consider when selecting linguistic structures for IE research. If acquisition is at least partially a result of how learners deal with input (hence the term input enhancement), it seems reasonable to look at structures not for structural properties alone but rather for potential problems related to their processing. To put this simply, *what is it about the processing of a structure that would make it easier or more difficult for an L2 learner?* It could be that a rule appearing to be easy in terms of the overt properties it exhibits may be difficult to process; conversely, a structure may look difficult from the outside but be easy to process. This of course begs the question of what processing is so I would like to touch on that matter before continuing with the question at hand.

By processing, I mean the moment-by-moment act of linking form and meaning or function during the act of comprehension. For example, for learners to get into their heads that English marks past tense overtly, they must consistently map the concept of PASTNESS onto the form –*ed* (as well as irregulars) as these forms are encountered in the input. For learners to get into their heads the differences between the copular verbs *ser* and *estar* in Spanish, they must consistently map the meanings associated with these copular verbs as they are encountered in the input. In short, there may be aspects of processing that we cannot readily determine merely by looking at overt properties of the grammar. We have to imagine what the processing mechanisms are, how they work, and then ask how these aspects of processing interact with structural difficulty/complexity if at all.

Now, back to how linguistic structure might make a difference. As mentioned before, the role of structure in the effectiveness of IE should hinge on how easy or difficult it is to process in the input. Some proposals have already been made in the literature in this regard, albeit not often considered by L2 researchers. O'Grady (2003), for example, suggests that distance between two elements makes a difference. Items that are co-referent or dependent on each other to comprehend well-formed utterances are more difficult to process the further they are from each other.

An alternative is that it is not just distance but syntactic boundaries across which information must be carried that makes the difference. Keating (2005), for example, suggests that processing difficulties increase not necessarily because of difference but because of the syntactic nodes between elements. Thus, it is easier to process co-referential grammatical structure in a noun phrase as opposed to when co-reference happens between two clauses or even two different phrases. He gives the example of gender agreement in Spanish. Mapping between adjective and noun in the same noun phrase (*la casa blanca*) is easier to process in the input than mapping across a clause (*la casa que mis padres pintaron blanca*). To be sure, structural properties themselves might form part of processing matters, but this will need to be sorted out.

In my own research, I have proposed a series of principles to suggest what underlying processing strategies learners might possess and how these interact with particular structures and form-meaning connections (e.g., VanPatten, 2004 and elsewhere). Factors that affect processing in my model are redundancy, whether or not forms actually encode meaning, and certain properties of word order.

Thus, as researchers seek to understand why IE sometimes does and sometimes does not make a difference, my argument is that they need to look at the processability of a structure as an intervening variable. This has been done with admirable ability by Pienemann (1998 and elsewhere), but his concern is not one of how mental representation develops but rather how language emerges in real time speech. We need to figure out, then, problems of processability during input processing.

Problems related to processability become even more evident in the research by Wong (2002). She demonstrated that input processed by learners as discrete sentences, as opposed to the same sentences assembled into a paragraph, led to greater learning. In short, working memory is taxed by processing both meaning and form; processing sentence by sentence is easier than processing a text when it comes to making form-meaning/function connections. Thus, at some level, processability for input may be tied into what can be held in working memory at any given moment (something that underlies the O'Grady and Keating positions described earlier as well as in my model of input processing).

Yet another way to look at the problem is this: are structures and forms distinguishable in terms of whether or not parsing is successful? In at least one scenario (Carroll, 2001 and elsewhere; L. White, 1987), acquisition proceeds only when parsing fails. By **parsing** we mean the moment by moment computation of sentence structure during the act of comprehension. During parsing, various levels of satisfaction or "fit" must be met or the parse "crashes." For example, let's say you hear "Yesterday John will go to the store." The adverb *yesterday* encodes for pastness and in English this pastness must match the verb inflection. It does not in our present example and as you read the sentence when you got to "will go" you probably shook your head and went "huh?" Your parser momentarily crashed. In an L2 scenario, if a learner's parser does not crash, then that means all computations were successful or at least the parser was satisfied with what went on or that information was dumped from working memory such that the parser didn't work on it anyway.

But note that "parsing failure triggers acquisition" is a real problem for acquisition: just how much "noise" can go by without the L2 learner's parser going "huh?" For this reason, learners miss a lot of data in the input early on because their parsers either cannot handle the information or merely don't process it. This is one explanation for why gender agreement between nouns and adjectives—a fairly simple and quite easy rule in the Romance languages—is acquired late or not acquired at all by learners coming from languages in which gender agreement is non-existent. For these learners, their L1 parsers do not have "built in expectations" that nouns and adjectives have to agree and thus no crash happens when, say, a feminine noun appears in the same sentence with a masculine adjective. They cannot transfer anything from the L1 to help processing so they are faced with waiting for the parser to crash in order to detect a potential learning problem. But a chicken and egg scenario is set up: in the case of adjective agreement, how do you get something into the parser so that there is a crash when you never detect it in the input to begin with? This is a profound problem, indeed, but one that takes us away from the topic at hand: defining difficulty in terms of processing. For a researcher like Carroll (2001), difficulty is thus defined in terms of *not* causing parsers to crash while at the same time being something that exists in the input. Thus, for her adjective agreement is an extremely difficult L2 phenomenon not in terms of structural features but in terms of parsing/processing problems (i.e., whether or not parsing failure occurs so that acquisition can be triggered).

Processing, of course, may involve salience as well. In my model of input processing, position within an utterance makes a difference in terms of likelihood that learners will detect a particular structure/form sooner or later compared to another structure/form. But salience is not without problems, as Kreuz and Caucci (this volume) point out and as Overstreet (this volume) demonstrates. Because salience is often defined after the fact (e.g., something may not be salient if it is difficult to acquire) or because salience is vaguely defined to begin with and there is sometimes disagreement on just what the properties of salience are, salience as a feature of processing does not lend itself well to selecting linguistic structures for IE research.

To summarize, what I am proposing for IE research thus far is the following:

- that we establish processing criteria that can be used to categorize aspects of language into distinct processing problems and thus degrees of difficulty or at least categories of easy/difficult and maybe impossible (i.e., structures that IE cannot possibly help);
- that we systematically investigate the impact that IE has on distinct types of processing problems.

I do not mean to suggest that we abandon structural complexity altogether as a variable in research; I am suggesting that it be tested right along with issues in processing so that over time we can sort out the most productive avenues to determine the *what* of IE as well as the *why*.

Explicit Information

Explicit information refers to the provision of explanation about how a structure "works" prior to treatment (activities). In research on IE, there has been considerable effort spent in examining whether or not explicit information helps acquisition, again with conflicting findings. For example, prior to activities to work with *–ing* in English, a researcher might give one group an explanation on the nature and use of this structure while a second group does not get the explanation, the idea being to investigate whether the explicit information helps at all.

In contradistinction to the position held by some researchers, it seems to me that investigating the presence or absence of explicit information and concluding that explicit information helps for the acquisition of some features and not others (at least via IE) may not hold water in the long run. To refresh our memories, there is research within IE that shows that explicit information provided prior to treatment results in more learning (as measured by certain tests) for some structures compared to others. There are three problems here. One is that we are left with no explanation as to why. A second problem is that certain post-treatment measurements of learning may not draw upon newly acquired/developing competence (residing in the mental representation) at all. The third problem involves the use of off-line research designs. Again, I will take each point separately.

That explicit information is useful for some structures as opposed to others is a descriptive statement and not an explanation. Why, for example, should learners benefit from having X explained to them but not Y before they engage in some kind of IE treatment? Some have attempted to answer this question in terms of structural properties, for example, defining easy structures in one way and difficult structures in another as we saw earlier as in deGraff's study. Yet the research does not always support the proposed ease/difficulty of a structure and some researchers show surprise when greater gains in development are demonstrated with a more difficult structure or when a simple structure seems to lag behind. Even if the research eventually demonstrated that explicit information works better with simple structures as opposed to more difficult ones (or vice versa, for that matter), we have no explanation for why. What exactly does explicit information do such that one type of structure is affected but not another?

In one interesting study, Fernández (2005) compared the acquisition of the Spanish subjunctive to word order and object pronouns as learners engaged in structured input activities (see Farley, 2005; Lee & VanPatten, 2003; Wong, 2004a). Each structure was crossed with the variable of explicit information so that four groups were compared: (1) subjunctive + explicit information, (2) subjunctive - explicit information, (3) word order/object pronouns + explicit information, (4) word order/object pronouns - explicit information. As participants performed the activities via computer, a program tracked their answers to examine how many trials (items) it took before learners began to perform correctly. What she found was a clear effect for the explicit information on the subjunctive but none for word order and object pronouns. That is, those who received explicit information prior to structured input activities with the subjunctive demonstrated fewer trials to criterion than those who did not get explicit information. However, those who received explicit information prior to structured input activities with word order and object pronouns did not reveal any advantage. For Fernández, however, there was no structural explanation for her results and instead she posited that there was a difference in learning to process the structures in the input that yielded the differential results. For the subjunctive, learners needed to apply an existing processing strategy to a new feature. This strategy already existed in their L1 and they had also been using it on other structures in their L2. The explicit information "primed" the re-application of the strategy. However, for word order and object pronouns, no prior processing mechanism or strategy existed—either in the L1 or the L2. Thus, learners had to "build" a new strategy and thus explicit information was less likely to help. In short, if you can use existing processing procedures and strategies, then explicit information is more likely to help than if you have to build new processing procedures and strategies. The latter will respond only to examples in the input (coupled with feedback, of course, regarding whether you actually understood correctly what you were listening to). This is the closest we have come to any kind of processing explanation about why some things are more difficult than others when it comes to processing input data (see N. Ellis, 2003 and elsewhere, who has argued for a confluence of factors such as frequency, uniqueness, and so on).

 Even if we had some good hypotheses to test regarding the "why" of explicit information, a major problem still remains: the research methodology used to investigate the role of explicit information in IE. Here I am referring to how gains in knowledge are measured. The problem lies in that it is not clear at all that researchers are testing actual underlying mental representations as opposed to some kind of explicit knowledge. When researchers use discrete point tests and other kinds of measurements that allow for participants to call upon the explicit information they have learned as opposed to any internalized knowledge, we cannot be sure that any effects of explicit information on acquisition are being measured at all. For example, Alanen (1995) used the following kind of test (among others) to measure learner acquisition of Finish suffixes of location: Use the last word in brackets to form meaningful Finnish sentences so that all sentences contain a place expression...Example: *Banaani on* _____ (*banaani* 'banana' *bouli* 'bowl'). (adapted from p. 301). Clearly, this test can be accomplished using explicit knowledge and in fact, once I had read the descriptions of how Finnish suffixes worked I took the test myself without any input. It did not seem terribly difficult. To be sure, Alanen used other tests as well but it is not clear that these others (e.g., grammaticality judgement, rule statement test) also could not be performed by relying exclusively if not mostly on explicit knowledge. (See Doughty, 2003 for an in depth discussion of the problem with research design and assessment in instructed SLA more generally.)

The problem, of course, is that there is no clear link between learned explicit information and acquisition itself and indeed, it would seem from a good deal of the research and theory so far in SLA, that there is reason to doubt any kind of link at all. But again, this hypothesis can be tested—however, it is not adequately tested to date.

Another problem with the research on testing the role of explicit knowledge is the difference between off-line and on-line methodologies. Assuming that we had adequate measures of acquisition of grammatical structure that did not tap into explicit knowledge or that did not favor explicit knowledge (cf. Doughty, 2003) and assuming we were approaching the problem from a processing perspective as part of our explanatory framework, off-line measures might not reveal anything or might lead us to the wrong conclusion. For example, in deGraff's study, those who received explicit information prior to engaging in activities gained more (albeit not much) in terms of knowledge as measured by his various off-line tests. In contradistinction, VanPatten and Oikennon (1996) showed that the presence or absence of explicit information contributed little to nothing to the outcome of structured input as used in their research, a finding replicated in later research (e.g., Benati, 2004; Wong, 2004a). We could say that the differences were due to treatment type: deGraff used a mixture of activity types involving comprehension practice and output practice while VanPatten and the others used structured input as contained in processing instruction (Farley, 2005; Lee & VanPatten, 2003; Wong, 2004b). Given that the treatments are quite different, the effects or non-effects of explicit information could be due to how the treatments led learners to engage the input. However, Farley (2004) reports that explicit information made a difference in a study that replicated VanPatten and Oikennon's design but merely changed the structure; that is, those that got explicit information along with structured input activities made greater gains than those who did not get explicit information. Thus, his results resemble deGraff's. Yet, his treatment was radically different from deGraff's and very much resembled that used in the other studies just mentioned (i.e., those that used processing instruction and structured input). So, the treatment explanation is out when comparing the findings of deGraff with those of, say, VanPatten and Oikennon. Focusing solely on the studies that used structured input as the IE, why would we get one set of results in one study and another in the other studies when it comes to the effects of explicit information?

The answer may be that off-line measures may mask some effect for explicit information and how it interacts with linguistic structure. Recall the Fernández (2005) study in which learners were engaged in structured input activities with and without prior explicit information. She also included another independent variable in her study—linguistic structure—for which she had two levels of the variable: the subjunctive and word order/object pronouns (both in Spanish), selected due to the different processing problems they represented. What she found was that explicit information helped in terms of the subjunctive but not in terms of word order/object pronouns. But she did not find this via an off-line test after treatment. How she measured the effect of explicit information was this: the number of trials (items) learners had to complete before they began to get answers right. What she found was that even though all groups in the end acquired new knowledge and there was no difference among them, within the two groups learning the subjunctive explicit information got them to answer correctly sooner than if it were absent. Thus, it sped up acquisition but ultimately it was not necessary. However, this was the case only for the subjunctive. For word order/object pronouns, the presence/absence of explicit information prior to treatment did not get either group to perform correctly sooner than the other.

What this means then is that explicit information in the form of explanation prior to treatment can have a hidden effect if we limit ourselves to off-line measures and if we do not consider differences in structures due to processing. It would be wrong to conclude that explicit information is always beneficial and it would be wrong to conclude that explicit information is not beneficial given the current state of the research. What is needed is systematic research in which on-line measures are crossed with type of structure in order to tease out any effects for explicit information.

Once again, let me summarize the main points in this section.

- Explanation for the role of explicit information, if any, will need to be found in processing issues.
- Research methodology cannot rely on performance measures that easily invite the use of conscious or explicitly learned information.
- Research methodology needs to expand to include on-line measures to get at processes not revealed by paper and pencil or even oral post-tests.

Long-Term Effects

The research on instructed SLA is sadly lacking when it comes to empirical studies of long-term effects. Almost all research on instructed SLA (and thus on IE) tests only short-term gains. Typically, after a treatment period, a pre-test is given immediately. In some studies, a "delayed" post-test is given a week or so later. Only in a few studies do the researchers administer a delayed post-test of say one month. Although it would appear that if learners continue to demonstrate improved performance after one-month then they are likely to have retained something, the several studies that do indeed look at long-term results suggest otherwise.

Lightbown (1983) reported that one year after intense drilling and practice on certain forms, the effects of the instruction disappeared; the learners "reverted" to where they were prior to drilling and practice. Granted, this is not a study on IE as we understand it so let's turn to one other study. Spada and Lightbown (1993) reported that five-months after an instructional intervention involving WH-question formation, learners seemed to maintain the gains they made by the end of the intervention. However, there is a problem with this finding. During the five-month period from treatment to delayed post-test, learners continued to receive instruction and feedback on the targeted linguistic item. Thus, any long-term effects observed were not due to one particular intervention but to a continued and sustained type of intervention.

There is one study that is suggestive of long-term effects with an isolated intervention. In VanPatten and Fernández (2004), we reported the results of a study involving processing instruction (see Wong, this volume) in which a delayed post-test was administered eight months after treatment. During the intervening period, no instruction or feedback was given on the targeted item (word order and object pronouns in Spanish) or any related items (e.g., reflexive pronouns, indirect object pronouns). We found that on the delayed post-test learners still performed significantly better than they did prior to treatment; however, they did not perform as well as they did immediately after treatment. Thus, although there were long-term effects, they were attenuated.

The results of the previous three studies are basically all we know about long-term effects of any kind of instruction, let alone IE. It seems to me that given the problems in research design (i.e., Do our assessment measures actually test acquired knowledge?) coupled with the short-term nature of research on IE, we really can't say much about the overall effects of any kind of instruction. It could be that all effects disappear with time, unless the instruction and feedback are constant as in the case of the Spada and Lightbown study.

Why aren't there more long-term studies? We could discuss a range of possible explanations ranging from problems in research design (e.g., keeping a large enough pool of subjects over a long period of time) to sociological aspects of the profession (e.g., the need to publish encourages "quick and dirty" studies) to human behavior (e.g., we're lazy researchers!). No matter the reason, long-term studies cannot be seen as a luxury any longer. Long-term studies are a necessity. Without them, we cannot validate the claims of any research on IE.

The main of point of this section then is the following:
- We must build up a cadre of long-term studies on IE using as many of the techniques as possible in the research. Such research should be systematic and cross with the variables of linguistic structure and explicit information.

Conclusion

In this chapter, I have examined two critical variables in IE research that are often not adequately addressed or treated: linguistic structure (and how it is selected) and the role of explicit information (along with issues in research design and methodology). I also addressed the need for long-term studies. Until some of the issues discussed here are tackled in some systematic way, then my belief is that we will continue to spin our wheels in IE research with conflicting findings and an inability to arrive at sustainable conclusions. With this said, I do not mean to imply that the issues discussed in this chapter are the only issues to address in terms of a continued research agenda on IE. Clearly, this volume points to a number of issues that preoccupy the research currently. My point is this: if we take any one of those issues, to what extent has the research factored in or considered how linguistic structure interacts with that particular issue (and how) and how explicit information interacts if at all (and how)? In awareness research, for example, how are structures selected for the research design? If the effects of awareness in IE can be teased out (assuming this necessary), is awareness such an independent variable that its role does not change depending on linguistic structure, processing problem, and so on? In research on feedback in IE, the same kinds of questions could be posed, as can be for salience and any other factor. Indeed, as I mentioned at the outset, the fact that some types of IE may be better than others may owe itself to just how we tackle the issue of linguistic structure (i.e., how these are selected for treatment) and the methodology used in research.

Following is a list of the main points made in this chapter.

- We need to establish processing criteria that can be used to categorize aspects of language into distinct processing problems and thus degrees of difficulty or at least categories of easy/difficult and maybe impossible (i.e., structures that IE cannot possibly help).
- We must systematically investigate the impact that IE has on distinct types of processing problems.
- Explanation for the role of explicit information, if any, will need to be found in processing issues.
- Research methodology cannot rely on performance measures that easily invite the use of conscious or explicitly learned information.
- Research methodology needs to expand to include on-line measures

to get at processes not revealed by paper and pencil or even oral post-tests.
- We must build up a cadre of long-term studies on IE using as many of the techniques as possible in the research. Such research should be systematic and cross with the variables of linguistic structure and explicit information.

My argument is that by addressing these points, we will be better able to satisfactorily research the benefits, if any, of the various kinds of IE and why any particular kind of IE is beneficial.

Questions and Topics for Discussion

1) Examine 4-5 empirical studies of IE. How do the authors define acquisition? If they don't, can you infer their thoughts about acquisition from what they say?
2) VanPatten argues that linguistic structure might be an intervening variable in the research on IE. That is, conflicting results of research may be due to types of linguistic structure used in the various studies. Decide whether the following structures are similar in terms of their ease/difficulty in acquisition due to overt structural properties: third-person -*s* in English (e.g., drinks, eats), regular plural markers in English (e.g., dogs, cats), and contracted copular for the third person (e.g., He's tall, Mary's liberal).
3) In one theory, difficulty of a structure may be due to processing distance. If things "have to agree" in a sentence, it is more difficult to acquire them if there is distance between the two things that must agree. Examine the three structures in #2 above and see if you can determine what differences in processing ease/difficulty exist for them.
4) It seems common sense that explicit information would help learners acquire features of language, yet the research in IE does not bear this out. Can you think of any arguments why explicit information would not be useful (other than, of course, providing a bad explanation)?
5) Why is the type of assessment in IE research so important to understanding the findings in the field?
6) With the little we know about long-term effects of IE, why are the results of current research suspect or at least need to be interpreted with caution?

References

Alanen, R. (1995). Input enhancement and rule presentation in second language acquisition. In R. Schmidt (Ed.), *Attention and awareness in foreign language acquisition* (pp. 259-302). Honolulu: University of Hawai'i Press.

Benati, A. (2004). The effects of structured input activities and explicit information on the acquisition of the Italian future tense. In B. VanPatten (Ed.), *Processing instruction: Theory, research, and commentary* (pp. 207-225). Mahwah, NJ: Lawrence Erlbaum.

Carroll, S. (2001). *Input and evidence: The raw material of second language acquisition*. Amersterdam: John Benjamins.

Corder, S.P. (1969). The significance of learners' errors. *International Review of Applied Linguistics, 5,* 161-170.

deGraff, R. (1997). *Differential effects of explicit instruction on second language acquisition*. Holland Institute of General Linguistics.

Doughty, C. (2003). Instructed SLA: Constraints, compensation, and enhancement. In C. Doughty & M. Long (Eds.), *Handbook of second language acquisition* (pp. 256-310). Oxford: Blackwell Publishing.

Doughty, C., & Long, M. (2003). *The handbook of second language acquisition*. Oxford: Blackwell.

Ellis, N. (2003). Constructions, chunking, and connectionism: The emergence of second language structure. In C. Doughty & M. Long (Eds.), *Handbook of second language acquisition* (pp. 63-103). Oxford: Blackwell Publishing.

Ellis, R. (1994). *The study of second language acquisition*. Oxford: Oxford University Press.

Farley, A. (2004). Processing instruction and the Spanish subjunctive: Is explicit information needed? In B. VanPatten (Ed.), *Processing instruction: Theory, research, and commentary* (pp. 227-239). Mahwah, NJ: Lawrence Erlbaum.

Farley, A. (2005). *Structured input: Grammar instruction for the acquisition oriented classroom*. New York: McGraw Hill.

Fernández, C. (2005). *The role of explicit information in processing instruction: An on-line experiment*. Unpublished doctoral dissertation. The University of Illinois at Chicago.

Gass, S., & Selinker, L. (2001). *Second language acquisition: An introductory course*. Mahwah, NJ: Lawrence Erlbaum.

Hulstijn, J. (1995). Not all grammar rules are equal: Giving grammar instruction its proper place in foreign language teaching. In R. Schmidt (Ed.), *Attention and awareness in foreign language acquisition* (pp. 359-386). Honolulu: University of Hawai'i Press.

Keating, G. (2005). *Processing gender agreement across phrases in Spanish: Eye movements during sentence comprehension.* Unpublished doctoral dissertation. The University of Illinois at Chicago.

Krashen, S. (1982). *Principles and practice in second language acquisition.* London: Pergamon.

Lee, J.F., & VanPatten, B. (2003). *Making communicative language teaching happen.* New York: McGraw-Hill.

Lightbown, P. (1983). Exploring relationships between developmental and instructional sequences in L2 acquisition. In H. Seliger & M. Long (Eds.), *Classroom oriented research* (pp. 217-243). Rowley, MA: Newbury House.

Long, M. (1983). Does second language instruction make a difference? A review of research. *TESOL Quarterly, 17,* 359-382.

O'Grady, W. (2003). The radical middle: Nativism without universal grammar. In C. Doughty & M. Long (Eds.), *Handbook of second language acquisition* (pp. 43-62). Oxford: Blackwell Publishing.

Pienemann, M. (1998). *Language processing and second language development.* Philadelphia: John Benjamins.

Robinson, P. (1995). Aptitude, awareness, and the fundamental similarity of implicit and explicit second language learning. In R. Schmidt (Ed.), *Attention and awareness in foreign language acquisition* (pp. 303-358). Honolulu: University of Hawai'i Press.

Spada, N., & Lightbown, P. (1993). Instruction and the development of questions in L2 classrooms. *Studies in Second Language Acquisition, 15,* 205-224.

VanPatten, B. (2004). Input processing in second language acquisition. In B. VanPatten (Ed.), *Processing instruction: Theory, research, and commentary* (pp. 5-31). Mahwah, NJ: Lawrence Erlbaum.

VanPatten, B., & Fernández, C. (2004). The long-term effects of processing instruction. In B. VanPatten (Ed.), *Processing instruction: Theory, research, and commentary* (pp. 273-289). Mahwah, NJ: Lawrence Erlbaum.

VanPatten, B., & Oikennon, S. (1996). Explanation vs. structured input in processing instruction. *Studies in Second Language Acquisition, 18,* 495-510.

White, J. (1998). Getting the learners' attention: A typographical input enhancement study. In C. Doughty & J. Williams (Eds.), *Focus on form in classroom second language acquisition* (pp. 85-113). Cambridge: Cambridge University Press.

White, L. (1987). Against comprehensible input: The input hypothesis and the development of second language competence. *Applied Linguistics, 8,* 95-110.

White, L. (2003). *Second language acquisition and universal grammar.* Cambridge: Cambridge University Press.

Wong, W. (2000). *The effects of textual enhancement and simplified input on L2 comprehension and acquisition of non-meaningful grammatical form.* Unpublished doctoral dissertation, the University of Illinois at Urbana-Champaign.

Wong, W. (2002). *Enhancing the learner's attention: A study with textual enhancement, orientation, and sentence- and discourse-level input.* Unpublished manuscript.

Wong, W. (2004a). Processing instruction in French: The roles of explicit information and structured input. In B. VanPatten (Ed.), *Processing instruction: Theory, research, and commentary* (pp. 187-218). Mahwah, NJ: Lawrence Erlbaum.

Wong, W. (2004b). The nature of processing instruction. In B. VanPatten (Ed.), *Processing instruction: Theory, research, and commentary* (pp. 33-63). Mahwah, NJ: Lawrence Erlbaum.

Wong, W. (2005). *Input enhancement: From theory and research to the classroom.* New York: McGraw-Hill.

www.ingramcontent.com/pod-product-compliance
Lightning Source LLC
Chambersburg PA
CBHW050801160426
43192CB00010B/1597